DISCARDED

The Decline of the Individual

Mark D. White

The Decline of the Individual

Reconciling Autonomy with Community

Mark D. White
Department of Philosophy
College of Staten Island/CUNY
Staten Island
NY, USA

ISBN 978-3-319-61749-7   ISBN 978-3-319-61750-3 (eBook)
DOI 10.1007/978-3-319-61750-3

Library of Congress Control Number: 2017944704

© The Editor(s) (if applicable) and The Author(s) 2017
This work is subject to copyright. All rights are solely and exclusively licensed by the Publisher, whether the whole or part of the material is concerned, specifically the rights of translation, reprinting, reuse of illustrations, recitation, broadcasting, reproduction on microfilms or in any other physical way, and transmission or information storage and retrieval, electronic adaptation, computer software, or by similar or dissimilar methodology now known or hereafter developed.
The use of general descriptive names, registered names, trademarks, service marks, etc. in this publication does not imply, even in the absence of a specific statement, that such names are exempt from the relevant protective laws and regulations and therefore free for general use.
The publisher, the authors and the editors are safe to assume that the advice and information in this book are believed to be true and accurate at the date of publication. Neither the publisher nor the authors or the editors give a warranty, express or implied, with respect to the material contained herein or for any errors or omissions that may have been made. The publisher remains neutral with regard to jurisdictional claims in published maps and institutional affiliations.

Cover credit: Cover design by Samantha Johnson

Printed on acid-free paper

This Palgrave Macmillan imprint is published by Springer Nature
The registered company is Springer International Publishing AG
The registered company address is: Gewerbestrasse 11, 6330 Cham, Switzerland

To my parents, who taught me always to question everything and everyone.

Acknowledgements

I thank Sarah Lawrence and Allison Neuburger at Palgrave Macmillan for helping me realize this final book in my "tryptrych" on the individual and society, following *The Manipulation of Choice* and *The Illusion of Well-Being*, and I thank Palgrave Macmillan in general for allowing me to do them all in the way I envisioned. (A note to the studio: When you make these three books into movies, I want this one split into two parts, just like *Twilight*!)

I also thank my good friends who stuck with me through the writing process, chief among them Bill Irwin, Lauren Hale, Carol Borden, Anita Leirfall, and Heidi Page. If not for their constant support and encouragement, you would not be reading this book today. (And did you really want to read *Twilight* again?)

Finally, I thank David Brooks, who got my dander up and inspired me to write this book. Although he ended up having the smaller role than I imagined at the outset, I might not have written it at all without him, and for that I am grateful.

Contents

1 Introduction — 1

2 The Individual in Psychology, Neuroscience, and Economics — 7

3 Big Data, Algorithms, and Quantification — 39

4 Individual in Essence, Social in Orientation — 71

5 Balancing the Individual and Society in Law and Politics — 107

6 Conclusion — 149

Index — 153

CHAPTER 1

Introduction

It seems that every day you can open your Web browser, or pick up a newspaper or magazine, and read a new article about how our brains are not as great as we thought at making good choices, and as a result, we make bad decisions that have a negative impact on our happiness, well-being, and success. It might be a report from a team of experimental psychologists showing how our choices are influenced by irrelevant factors (such as the color of the room we are in) or how our decisions about the future change as the future gradually becomes the present (such as scheduling a painful medical procedure for three months from now but then canceling three days before). Sometimes, it is a new study from neuroscientists that shows how our brains get more fatigued in certain decision-making contexts or that making choices in some situations lights up the same parts of our brains that light up in other, wildly different situations, making us question just how rational and deliberate we really are.

After reading enough of these articles, it is only natural to question your own decision-making abilities. There are several ways you can react to this. You may take steps to try to counter these cognitive shortcomings: For instance, after reading about unconscious bias, you may try harder to overcome it on a conscious level, checking your intuitive judgments of people for any sign of prejudice. Or, you might seek out help making better decisions: After reading about problems of maintaining willpower in stressful circumstances, for example, you might enlist friends or support groups to help you keep on track with your long-term plans.

Regardless of how you react to these reports, some other people read them and conclude that whether they know it or not, individuals need help making better decisions. Furthermore, these people take it on themselves to help, based on their idea of what individuals really want or need and the choices they would make if only they could make better decisions. When these people are in positions of political influence, this impulse can often result in paternalistic policies. Sometimes, these are of the classic type in which certain choices are banned or taxed, but more recently, they are of the "nudge" variety, in which subtle changes to choice situations are designed to steer individuals' decisions in the direction the policymaker believes is in the individuals' interests.

Policymakers have always had some paternalistic tendencies, but the justification for these policies has changed in recent years. Whereas the government used to ban certain goods or services for moralistic or puritanical reasons, to craft more upstanding community members or citizens, today it is more often done, not to change who individuals are or what they want to do, but to help them make better choices in their interests, motivated by the flawed decision-making faculties described in psychological and neuroscientific studies.

I talked about these policy issues in an earlier book, *The Manipulation of Choice*, but this is just the beginning to a much broader argument. In this book, I will explain why the new "libertarian paternalism" and the science it is based on are but one example of a slow but steady *decline in respect for the individual*. I believe this decline could be catastrophic for all of us as individuals and as a society, and it results from a grievous misunderstanding of what the individual is and can be. This is not an argument for the individual versus society, but how the individual can be conceived as a part of society while still being an individual.

What are other signs of this decline? In another recent book, *The Illusion of Well-Being*, I explored the academic and policymaking trend of happiness studies, which is similar to nudge paternalism in that it seems to respect individuals' conceptions of their interests and what comprises their happiness, but actually has policymakers making these decisions for individuals and then influencing their decisions in that direction. This is another example of the devaluation of individuals' choices, their interests, and—specifically in this case—their ideas of their own happiness in favor of externally imposed versions. These imposed conceptions of individuals' happiness are too vague and general to represent the thoughts and feelings of any one person; nonetheless, it is this vision of happiness that guides policy that influences our choices and the paths of our lives.

Another example comes from the realm of data science: the ongoing trend toward quantification of everyday life as represented by Big Data and algorithms. As computing power develops and becomes more accessible, and the cost of data storage falls to negligible levels, we have started measuring and tracking everything about our lives: how many steps we walk, how many minutes we spend online, and how many grams of sugar we eat. Of course, we are not the only ones measuring tracking what we do: Businesses such as Amazon and Netflix famously track all our buying and watching habits and then offer suggestions that are tailored to our tastes as expressed through our behavior. Finally—and perhaps most controversially—governments track much of what we do, not only through online data but also through video and audio surveillance, and use that information to predict who is more likely to commit criminal or terrorist acts.

As with nudge and happiness policy, we all too easily fall for the lure of the quantified self. We enjoy tracking so many statistics relevant to our lives and often make good use of them, especially to counter weakness of will that stands in the way of achieving goals and finishing projects. But as I described, other parties also use this information for their own purposes, some which align with our own goals and some which do not. In general, it's the process of quantification, rather than who does it and why, that is of concern: The fact that collapsing so much of life's complexity into numbers and trends, and then tracking them over time and processing their through algorithms to generate future plans, erodes the rich uniqueness of each individual. When you reduce people to numbers, you render them comparable and exchangeable, and you risk forgetting they are individuals and not simply members of a set. This contributes to the decline in respect for the individual and the promotion of the whole (the sum or average of the numbers) in his or her stead.

While the developments above are ultimately grounded in breaking developments in psychology, neuroscience, and technology—which are fascinating and invaluable in their own right, aside from how they are used by government, business, or us—the value of the individual has also been questioned by more humanistic thinkers writing from the viewpoints of philosophy, sociology, and politics. Such writers often depict the individual as isolated, asocial, and selfish, unable to think of anyone but themselves, thereby endangering the social fabric that sustains us all. Based on this caricature of an individual—and the depiction of modern society as "radically individualistic" that follows from it—these commentators recommend shifting emphasis and power from individuals, who make bad decisions, to society (or the state), who, it is assumed, would make better ones.

What both of these groups, the scientists and the humanists, have in common is their doubts about the competence of the individual. Specifically, those working from psychology, neuroscience, and data science question the *cognitive competence* of the individual, while those on the more humanistic side doubt the *moral competence* of the individual.

They are both wrong, however, and for similar reasons. Every day, psychology and neuroscience are revealing more and more about how we make decisions, but they cannot say anything about *why* we make them—the interests, goals, and dreams that motivate the decisions themselves. Without this knowledge, scholars and policymakers must assume certain interests on the part of individuals, and it is based on those interests that they feel justified to judge certain decisions as wrong, misguided, or suboptimal.

Furthermore, they work with an extremely simplified picture of human choice, assuming one very general interest at a time and assuming all decisions must further this interest…or else it is a bad decision. Eating a muffin? That doesn't further your health, so it's a bad decision. Not maxing out your retirement account contributions? That doesn't further your savings, so it's a bad decision. Not spending enough time with friends? That doesn't maximize your happiness, so it's a bad decision. There is no accounting for the complexity of individual choice and interests, and it's all too easy to decide for themselves that an individual is making bad choices when judged against a single interest that has little to do with how they made them.

Just as those working from science are using an oversimplified idea of human faculties of decision-making, those on the humanities side have an oversimplified idea of how individuals think about themselves and the people around them. They present an extreme distinction between the individual, selfish and alone, and a tight-knit society, in which we are all tightly bonded and supportive of each other. Either you're *you* or you're one of *us*… but you can't be both. This distinction is a false dichotomy and a pernicious one at that, and in this book, I present a better way to think about the individual.

I will argue that each of us is *individual in essence, social in orientation*. Inspired by the moral philosophy of Immanuel Kant, I will explain that we are by nature separate persons, making our own independent choices, but for a wide variety of different reasons, many of which are inherently social or other-regarding. I can make a decision as an individual to work with others or help others or follow the lead of others—but each is my decision. An individual can be the most community-minded, altruistic, and social person in the world, but he or she is still making those decisions as an individual. Individuals working together as a group to do great things are still *individuals working together*. It is not one or the other, individual or social—it can be both and it usually *is* both.

This false picture of the individual in relation to society is not simply of academic interest; if it were, I would be writing this book for fellow academics, not a broader audience. It speaks to the nature of a liberal society that balances the rights of each individual with the concerns of the whole. This balance is the core of liberal government, as represented by its greatest thinkers, such as John Stuart Mill and Immanuel Kant, and as enshrined in the Bill of Rights to the US Constitution. And it is endangered by a mind-set that gradually erodes our appreciation of the cognitive and moral competence of the individual—indeed, the relevance, importance, and value of each of us—and elevates the whole, which can lead to utilitarian decision-making that dismisses the rights and dignity of the individual in favor of the "big picture" and "getting things done." We will see this trend in a number of recent government policies and Supreme Court decisions, some of which affirm the value of the individual but many which unfortunately do not.

This book is an attempt to restore a nuanced idea of the individual that is both cognitively and morally competent and deserving of the respect that modern liberal societies have traditionally given it. I'm not arguing for an individualistic society or a "radical individualism" or any sort. I prefer to think of us as a society of individuals living together, working together, and achieving great things together, while at the same remaining unique and autonomous persons. We can promote the goals of all while maintaining respect for the rights and interests of each individual, and it starts with recognizing our own value, worth, and dignity as individuals—and then forcing our elected leaders to do the same.

CHAPTER 2

The Individual in Psychology, Neuroscience, and Economics

As we start our exploration of the decline in respect for the individual, we'll begin with the way we think about how we think. Understanding how human beings make decisions has puzzled our greatest philosophers and scientists for thousands of years, and we still struggle with it today, despite advances in these fields. In particular, fascinating developments in psychology and neuroscience over the last several decades have shed light on some unexpected quirks in our decision-making processes which steer our choices away from what would seem rational or prudent. Many of these quirks help explain why some of us eat too much, exercise too little, or spend our money on things we want now instead of saving it for things we will need in the future.

The evidence pouring out from the laboratories of psychologists and neuroscientists on almost a daily basis can easily make us doubt our own decision-making abilities. And certainly, we all make some dumb choices from time to time (I doubt it's just me!). However, these scientific findings —especially as reported by a media environment that oversimplifies the nuance and detail of experimental science and amplifies the most sensational results—can lead to think we make bad choices all the time. Furthermore, it isn't just the way these results are presented: The way that experiments are designed, conducted, and interpreted by scientists themselves also contributes to an overly pessimistic view of our faculties of choice.

In this chapter, we'll look at how scientists think about choice and then consider a more elaborate, nuanced, and inclusive understanding of it. We'll talk about how researchers' preconceptions about choice affect the way they interpret their experimental findings and how this filters down to our own perceptions of our decision-making as well as how others see it. Businesses and government have their own reasons to understand how we make decisions too, and these understandings affect how they behave toward us when trying to influence our decisions. Given the coercive nature of state power, such influence is more troubling when practiced by the government, even if this is well-intentioned. All of this culminates in the first step in the overall argument of this book: that respect for the individual is being eroded, a trend we need to acknowledge and understand, so we can begin to reverse it.

The Choices We Make, for Better or for Worse

We make many choices throughout a normal day. Some are so trivial and automatic that they don't deserve to called choices at all. For example, when I put my shoes on, I usually put the left one on first. I don't make a conscious choice to start with my left shoe each and every time I put my shoes on—I just do. My "decision" to put my shoes on in the first place is not much of a choice either; before I go out, I put on shoes. If there is any true choice involved, it would be which shoes to wear (which, for me, is never much of a decision either).

These are routine choices to which we don't give much thought, if any. But many of our choices, even minor ones, *are* true choices: what to wear for the day, what to eat (or where to go) for lunch, or which project to work on today. Then, there are the more significant choices: which online match to message for a date, which book to read (after you're done with this one, of course), or which car to buy. Finally, we have the "big ones," decisions such as which person to commit to, which job to take, and where to live. These decisions can be so monumental in the context of a life that they influence each other: For example, an attractive new job may be in a different city or country than you (and our significant other) want to live.

How do we make all of these decisions? It is reasonable to assume that our choices are made with a goal in mind. Sometimes, our goal is clear. If you want a burger for lunch (a common goal of mine), you choose a place that sells burgers; you would hardly further this goal by going to a sushi restaurant. But let's say you not only want a burger, but also want to go to a place that is quiet, close to work, not too unhealthy, within a certain price range, and without that thick mustard that always gives you an upset stomach around three in the afternoon. That is a much more complicated goal (or set of goals). If there is one place that fits all those criteria, then congratulations, your choice is made. If there is more than one, then you can introduce other criteria as well: For instance, maybe you just went to one of them last week, so you go to another one now (And please tell me where you live).

More likely, there is no one burger joint that meets all of these criteria. Then, you have to decide which aspects of a burger place, or which one of your goals regarding lunch, are more important to you. Is quiet more important than cost? Is health more important than proximity to work? If you are strapped for cash this week, cost may be the overriding factor, but if you just saw your cardiologist yesterday, you may have your health on your mind. And some days, for some reason, you just really want that thick mustard. (The mouth wants what it wants, even if the stomach disagrees.)

If deciding on a place for lunch can be this complicated—especially if we lay out all the various aspects of the decision—you can imagine how complex our decisions are when they are about which job to take, where to live, and who to commit to. When facing choices like these in the past, you may have drawn up lists of pros and cons, and maybe they went on for pages. There's a lot involved in these choices, and for good reason: they will have an immeasurable impact on your life going forward. Even if there is no right or wrong choice, and no one choice can be said to be better than another, each will result in a different path for your life in many important ways, and you are right to spend time trying to predict what these paths will look like.

However, in decisions as big as these, and even in smaller ones like picking somewhere to eat lunch, we often are not aware of all the factors that go into the decision, much less what factors are more important at the time than others. We go with our gut, so to speak, and make the choice that has the most appeal, the one that we are happy with. (It may not even the best decision you could have made; if you take the time necessary to choose *the* perfect place for lunch, you might not get there before dinner.) We're usually confident that we did have reasons to make the choice we did, and if we thought long enough we could probably articulate a fair number of them. But at a certain level, our choice is intuitive; we make the decision that furthers our goals—or, more generally, our *interests*—whether conscious or not.

Of course, not all of these decisions will be good ones. We have all made boneheaded choices from time to time, some of them more significant than others. Choosing the burger joint with the heavy mustard is a small mistake, but marrying the wrong person is not. But let's not be too hard on ourselves. Some decisions do not turn out the way we wanted them to, but this does not mean our decision-making process is at fault. If you choose a certain route to drive to work, and then traffic comes to a sudden stop because of an eight-car pile-up a mile up the road, you'll wish you would chosen another route. But there was no way to know that accident would happen, so you can't blame your decision-making process; you made the best choice with the information you had at the time.

The cases in which we can legitimately say we made a bad decision are those in which we made them the wrong *way*. We can often pick out some step in our decision-making process in that particular case that went askew and led to a bad outcome. Maybe we weren't careful enough, such as when we neglect to check the traffic report before choosing a route to get to work, or when we buy a new TV without reading any reviews first. Maybe we were unduly swayed by clever advertising to order those new honey-glazed ribs even though eating honey-glazed ribs makes the heavy mustard seem like apple juice. And maybe we drunk-texted that ex at four in the morning because… well, because we were drunk. (Oops.) In all of these cases, not only was the outcome unfortunate (if not painful), but the bad outcomes resulted from faulty decision-making: We "should have known better."

The examples I gave above are fairly trivial, but bad decisions can have much more serious effects that are definitely no joke. Even minor choices, each of which has little impact in the here and now, can lead to significantly negative outcomes over time. Everyone who has struggled with addiction to alcohol, cigarettes, or food knows this all too well; they fight the temptation to have "just one drink," or a cigarette or cookie, every day. In the same way, financial decisions made against the background of insufficient information or emotional turmoil may have a negative impact on your income or wealth for years to come. And yes, even drunk-texting your ex could have catastrophic consequences, especially if you do it while you are in a relationship with someone else. (Big oops.)

Enter the Psychologists and Neuroscientists

We're not the only people concerned about our bad decisions. Scholars, writers, poets, and songwriters have been musing for thousands of years about how and why we make the choices we make. Among the scholars who study choice are psychologists, economists, and neuroscientists, who in the last half-century or so have been tremendously productive in finding specific instances and circumstances in which our choices are particularly likely to go wrong.

In the 1950s, Herbert Simon, a polymath who worked in many fields related to decision science such as psychology, computer science, and management studies, criticized the unrealistic models of human decision-making normally used in economics (a field in which he won the Nobel Prize in 1978). Economists have a very simplistic model of choice, embodied in the hypothetical decision-maker *homo economicus*, which they argue is the source of its wide applicability and predictive power. In this model, individuals faced with a choice are assumed to have all the necessary information, which they can process perfectly in terms of all of their wants and needs to arrive at *the* one option that gives them the most satisfaction they can achieve (given their available resources such as money and time). In essence, each individual is assumed to be a computer or, as the economist Thorstein Veblen captured it more elegantly, a "lightning calculator of pleasures and pains who oscillates like a homogeneous globule of desire of happiness under the impulse of stimuli that shift him about the area, but leave him intact."[1]

Simon suggested that rather than having "perfect rationality" as economic models usually assumed, human beings instead have *bounded rationality*.[2] In this model of decision-making, people take the best information they can get, and think about it as well as they can, to make the best choice they can make in the time they have. There are limitations on how well each stage of this process can be performed that mirror the real-life imperfections of human beings. And even though the resulting choice may not be the "perfect" choice that individuals would have made if they had complete information, a perfect ability to process it, and all the time in the world, it is *good enough*. In fact, even though we like to think of ourselves as trying to make the best decisions we can at every point in our lives, more often we are satisfied with decisions that are good enough. As opposed to the ideal of maximizing or optimizing with regard to decision-making, Simon called this *satisficing*: making a decision that is good enough (or satisfactory) given all the many constraints involved.[3]

Simon's work was a precursor to modern research in neuroscience that emphasizes the brain's natural limits on processing capacity.[4] At the risk of understatement, our brains are incredible, capable of amazing feats of intelligence, creativity, and kindness. But at the same time, they are biological organs evolved to promote survival and enable reproduction; they were not "designed" to excel at abstract thought and precise calculation. The fact that we can do these things at all is a testament to the adaptability of the human brain. But our brains did not evolve for this reason, and we should not be disappointed to learn that they do not follow the precise mathematical logic of "perfect rationality" in decision-making, nor do they always arrive at the same solutions to problems that perfect rational processes would suggest.

More recently, psychologists working in the area of decision-making have discovered more specific ways in which our rationality falls short of perfection, many of them predictable based on the particular circumstances or context of a choice situation. The most influential research in this area was conducted and published by Daniel Kahneman and Amos Tversky beginning in the 1970s.[5] Kahneman won the Nobel Prize in economics in 2002 for this work; Tversky, sadly, had passed before the award was given (but his contribution to their joint work was recognized in the prize announcement). Over the course of hundreds of experiments over several decades, Kahneman, Tversky, and many of their colleagues investigated specific "shortcuts" our brains take to save on the limited cognitive resources described above. Many of them evolved to enhance survival in more primitive times when quick decisions made the difference between life and death, and concerns about optimal choices for the long run did not seem as urgent.

Some of the more widely known biases, heuristics, and dysfunctions found by Kahneman and Tversky include:

Present bias: This describes our tendency to emphasize short-term benefits and costs to the exclusion of long-term ones. Present bias made a lot of sense when being closely attuned to the present was necessary to survive into the future, a situation most of us in the developed world do not often experience. Some preference for the present over the future is reasonable, because we don't know as much about ourselves or the state of the world the farther into the future we try to imagine and plan for. But if we assume we will probably exist in some form ten years from now, it would be prudent to take our future self's interests into account when making decisions now, such as those concerning diet, exercise, and finances. But present basis works again this, leading us to ignore our future selves completely, live entirely for the present, and have that extra donut, skip that physical, or spend all of that holiday bonus now.

Confirmation bias: This describes our tendency to pay more attention to, and give more weight to, new information that confirms what we already believe, and dismiss new information to the contrary. If you think bacon is the key to eternal life, you'll always remember that one article in *Car and Driver* that promoted mass bacon consumption, while forgetting every study in the *New England Journal of Medicine* that cautions against it. This bias re-enters the public consciousness every election season—or, as we call it these days, "all the time"—because of our tendency to watch news channels and read newspapers or websites that correspond to our political beliefs, which serves to reinforce and strengthen those beliefs instead of challenging them and exposing us to other points of view.[6] Researchers think confirmation bias may have evolved to allow people to win arguments more often by enabling them to marshal supporting evidence quickly, but this comes at the expense of gathering more accurate information to make the best decisions for oneself.[7]

Availability heuristic: A close relative of confirmation bias and a cornerstone of bounded rationality, the availability heuristic describes our tendency to be satisfied with new information that is easy to obtain even if it might not be the most accurate or complete. Again, when our ancestors had to assess a dangerous situation with a predator very quickly, it made sense to rely on the information at hand because there was no time to get more. We may have much more time to make decisions these days, but we also have far more information at our fingertips, much more than we can possibly process in a reasonable amount of time. As a result, we often simply take the first bit of news we can get, whether through Facebook, Twitter, or our preferred news site or channel, regardless of whether that is the most accurate or truthful news out there.[8]

There are many more examples, but you get the idea.[9] All of these cognitive quirks are departures from our idealized preconceptions of how we should make decisions; while they may have been prudent and even life-preserving many thousands of years ago, these biases and heuristics now pose problems when they interfere with what should be more considered decisions in our long-term interests.

A more familiar example may be our evolved taste for fatty foods. When we were not sure when we would have a chance to eat again, they were calorie-rich sources for energy, but now they're a problem, especially in the developed world where food can be summoned with a swipe on our phones. Even our taste for sugar, now widely considered a greater threat to health than fat is, had a negligible effect when it was relatively rare; now that high-fructose corn syrup is in everything, our tastes are biting back against us.[10] We can resist our cravings for fatty and sugary foods (ha!) and even train ourselves to ignore them (ha ha!), but they are always there. In the same way, our cognitive biases, heuristics, and dysfunctions are, to a large extent, hardwired in our brains by thousands of years of evolution and have an undeniable effect on our decision-making processes.

In his 2011 book *Thinking, Fast and Slow*, Kahneman popularized many of his findings with Tversky and also introduced broader audiences to the ideas of System 1 and System 2 thinking.[11] *System 1* is the more reactionary, quick decision-making (that we often regret), while *System 2* is the more deliberate, measured type of thought that we usually think of as "rational." (Neuroscientists study the same dual levels of thinking in terms of *automatic* versus *controlled* processes, corresponding to Systems 1 and 2, respectively.) Most of the cognitive biases surveyed earlier operate by way of our System 1 thinking, our rapid responses to urgent choices. If we acknowledge these quirks, we can consciously try to overcome them by using our System 2 thinking, but at times when we have to make quick decisions (even if not life-and-death ones), it's hard for our System 1 thinking not to fall into these traps. In such situations, we might rely on easily available information, especially when it corresponds with our beliefs, and make a decision based on the now rather than the later, even though we know better.[12] It's just part of what we are as human beings who just recently arrived in the modern world after hundreds of thousands of years in the wilderness.

THE ECONOMISTS AND LAWYERS JOIN IN

All of these developments coming from psychology and neuroscience are tremendously informative and reveal valuable insights about the inner workings of our brains. They also emphasize, as I tried to do above, that our brains are not perfect computing machines but rather biological mechanisms that evolved to solve problems related to survival and reproduction. Unfortunately, many who interpret and use these findings do so, not in the context of the natural development of the brain and we evolved to think, but in the context of their own ideas about how we *should* think: specifically, preconceived notions about perfect rationality. Even we ourselves tend to think we should be logical and rational in all of our choices, and so we take these scientific findings as challenges or criticisms of our decision-making processes rather than descriptions and may conclude that we're not as good at making choices as we "should" be.

Perhaps, the best example of this comes from economics, in terms of both theory and policy. The work of Kahneman and Tversky has spread beyond psychology to other fields, none with more impact than economics, where it helped launch the field of *behavioral economics*.[13] If these new findings were going to shake up any field, economics was the obvious one because of its adherence to a model of perfectly rational decision-making. And economists deserve credit for accepting, accommodating, and adapting to the new discoveries about how the brain works—not all economists, mind you, but enough of them to generate talk of whether behavioral economics is on its way to becoming, simply, economics.[14]

But many behavioral economists have taken an odd approach to appreciating the insights of the psychological work. Rather than taking this work as a challenge to the model of perfect rationality, which it shows to be a flawed and overly simplistic representation of our real-life decision-making, they take the position that human beings can be and *would be* perfectly rational if not for our evolved cognitive quirks, which are obstacles to reaching our full cognitive potential. In other words, for many behavioral economists, perfect rationality is the benchmark, and all the findings of experimental psychology are ways in which we fail to reach it. In discussing the assumptions (or *axioms*) of rational choice models, economists Glen Whitman and Mario Rizzo write that while "behavioral economics challenges the positive validity of those [rationality] axioms in describing human behavior," it "maintains those axioms as normative standards to which agents ought to conform."[15] To some behavioral economists, the mainstream economic models are not wrong—it is our brains that are wrong because they do not fit the models. As psychologist Gerd Gigerenzer writes, behavioral economists "rather uncritically accept the rules of [the standard model] as the norm for all rational behavior, and blame mortals for not living up to this ideal."[16]

Consistent with this emphasis on perfect rationality, legal scholars—especially those already using the tools of economics to analyze choices, rules, and outcomes in legal settings—began working with economists, psychologists, and neuroscientists, embracing behavioral economics and steering it in a more proactive direction.[17] Not only did they continue investigating the implications of Kahneman and Tversky's work for models of perfect rationality (especially in legal situations), but they also recommended new policies and laws that would help individuals in the real world counteract their cognitive biases and dysfunctions and make better decisions—that is, decisions closer to the decisions they would make if they were perfectly rational.

This movement reached its zenith with the publication of the book *Nudge* in 2008.[18] Written by behavioral economist Richard Thaler and legal scholar Cass Sunstein based on previous academic work, *Nudge* promised a new policy tool that would improve individuals' choices without controlling, blocking, or coercively affecting them. True to their title, they proposed the use of "nudges," small changes to a choice situation (or *choice architecture*) that would leverage individuals' cognitive biases and dysfunctions to help them make better choices in their own interests.

Thaler and Sunstein provide many examples of nudges in their book and subsequent work; I'll just mention two of the most prominent. The first deals with a choice many people make when they get a new job: whether to enroll in a retirement program such as a 401(k), which not only accrues interest tax-free but is often matched to a certain degree by the employer. Usually, the default choice is not to enroll, implying that new employees have to make an active choice to enroll. Thaler and Sunstein judge that too few new employees enroll, given the financial advantages, and therefore propose making enrollment the default choice, with the option to decline.[19] Like many other changes in default options suggested by Thaler and Sunstein, this nudge takes advantage of *status quo bias*—our tendency to accept the current state of affairs rather than to consider the consequences of an alternative choice—in order to increase retirement savings. Because we are likely to accept defaults without much rational consideration, Thaler and Sunstein argue that making enrollment the default will increase people's retirement savings while not blocking them from declining to enroll if they want.

The second example involves arranging the food items in a cafeteria to encourage healthier food choices among customers. Because our choices are influenced by how they're presented, Thaler and Sunstein propose that cafeteria managers arrange choices so that healthier options are easier to reach and displayed more prominently and attractively, thereby encouraging customers subtly to select them.[20] Specifically, this nudge leverages *framing effects*—the outsized influence that the presentation of options has on the eventual choices we make among them—to encourage better eating and health in general. By simply making the salads easier to reach and more brightly lit than the pudding, customers are more likely to choose the former, promoting their general health while not preventing them from indulging their sweet tooth.

An important aspect of a nudge is that it does not foreclose any choices: New employers are free to opt out of retirement programs and customers can still choose the fried chicken and carrot cake instead of the salad and fruit cup. Due to our hardwired inclination to accept defaults and choose more attractive options, however, these nudges make us more likely to choose options that policymakers believe are better for us (or the ones we would presumably choose in the absence of cognitive quirks that lead us astray). For this reason, Thaler and Sunstein call the nudge program "libertarian paternalism," a new, subtler type of paternalism that steers individuals' choices in directions judged to be in their interests while not blocking any choices altogether or significantly increasing their costs (such as by taxing them).[21] This idea has become very popular around the world, with the USA, the UK, and other countries establishing departments or initiatives to explore the use of nudging in policymaking.[22]

PROBLEMS IN THE LAND OF NUDGE

However well-intentioned, the concept of nudges involves serious problems that we can trace ultimately to the way economists and policymakers interpret the more basic psychological research that grounds it. To be more precise, there are two missing links in the chain from saying "some decisions are less than optimal" to "the government must act to improve individuals' decisions." Each of these missing links is problematic from either a logical or an ethical view, and both of them illustrate the decline in respect for the individual that is the larger point of this book.[23]

The first missing link is the generalization from "*some* of individuals' decisions in certain contexts are mistaken" to "*most or all* of individuals' decisions in certain contexts are mistaken." As we have seen, psychologists have shown that decisions are more likely to be compromised in certain contexts and situations. For example, "hot" choice situations that are emotionally intense or rushed, such as feeling forced to make a major purchase "while this once-in-a-lifetime offer lasts," are more likely to engage an individual's quick System 1 response without sufficient time for lengthy System 2 deliberation. This also applies to choice situations in which emotions are triggered more than facts or considered opinions, such as surprise marriage proposals (especially in public and *especially* on the Jumbotron at the playoffs). Also, decisions involving insufficient or unreliable information, or considerations of risk, also tend to make the best decisions less likely: Many financial decisions regarding borrowing or large purchases fit this characterization for many of us.[24]

The keywords here, however, are "more likely" and "less likely." Even if dumb choices are more common in some situations than others, not *every* decision made in less-than-perfect circumstances will be mistaken. When we make that improper jump in logic, however, we not only seem to justify more intervention in individuals' choices, but also cast doubt on their basic powers of decision-making in general.

What explains this logical jump? The answer combines two aspects of nudging: the preconceptions about choice held by economists and policymakers, and the limits on what aspects of behavior they can observe.

Above, we discussed the two ways we can think of our own choices as bad: judging the process and judging the outcome. Scholars and policymakers do the same thing: Either they decide that an individual's decision-making process is compromised by some cognitive dysfunction or quirk, or they judge the decision the individual actually makes to be bad or wrong.

If they decide that an individual's choice process is flawed, policymakers can design a policy to improve that process by counteracting the flaw. Common policies of this type include offering information to help people make better choices (either in System 2 thinking or to prompt that type of thinking), or enforcing "cooling-off periods," mandatory delays in implementing decisions, so people have some time to change their minds once they have had a chance to think about it. Because these nudges do not steer people toward a particular decision, but instead improve individuals' decision-making processes themselves, they will have little effect on those who would have made sound choices anyway. In sense, they exemplify the spirit of what Colin Camerer and his colleagues call *asymmetric paternalism*, which

> creates large benefits for those who make errors, while imposing little or no harm on those who are fully rational. Such regulations are relatively harmless to those who reliably make decisions in their best interest, while at the same time advantageous to those making suboptimal choices.[25]

Because of this, these more passive nudges are mostly unproblematic; even if scholars and policymakers are overly pessimistic or judgmental regarding individuals' decision-making processes, such nudges do not interfere with those decisions and may even help people with generally sound choice processes make better decisions on occasion.

More importantly, this type of nudge is not predicated on the judgment of the final choices individuals actually make. Unfortunately, the second basis for judging choices does exactly this, wherein policymakers observe individuals' decisions and decide that these decisions are not in their best interests. This reveals a much more serious problem regarding the concept of nudges and reflects how individuals' choices and interests are understood by scholars and policymakers alike.

Consider choices like the following: eating sugary foods, smoking cigarettes, living a sedentary lifestyle, not participating in a retirement program, neglecting one's studies, and ignoring current news events. We can think of any number of cognitive biases and dysfunctions to explain these, but this is not the reason we might suspect they're bad choices. If we question these choices, it is more likely because we suspect they're bad for the people making them: They will result in poor health, financial situation, educational outcomes, or civic participation.

This is a reasonable suspicion, but we must also acknowledge that it's only a guess based on *our ideas* of what is best of the people making these choices. We may see an overweight man eating a banana split and think that was a bad decision, but we can't *know* it was a bad decision—that is for him alone to say because he alone knows why he made it. We may hear that the new assistant in our office declined to enroll in the firm's retirement program and think that was wrong, but we can't *know* it was wrong—she may have had valid reasons to put off enrollment.

In other words, we don't know why other people make the choices they make, because we don't know the *interests* in which they make them. The man eating the banana split may be rewarding himself for a year of sustained weight loss, or for a promotion he worked very hard to get, or simply because he really wanted one, in full knowledge of the adverse effects on his health. The new employee who declined the retirement program may be saving money for a down payment on a house, sending money to her parents to help with their medical bills, or planning a huge blowout in Vegas with her friends. We may not agree with these reasons, but they're not for us to judge, not if we want to respect individuals and their own goals and interests.

Policymakers are in the same situation when they observe and judge other people's choices: They have no knowledge of the interests in which these decisions are made and, therefore, no way to know whether these decisions advance those interests. Instead, they use their own idea of what individuals' interests are—or what they feel individuals' interests *should* be—and judge their choices against it. You and I may do the same thing casually, of course, but we do not have the power to implement policy to change decisions we judge to be wrong (if we wanted to). And it isn't just the more active nudges that are based on this presumption: The passive nudges such as education and cooling-off periods are also based on a judgment of poor choices in the hope that decision-makers will make a better choice under better conditions (even if no alternative choice is actively nudged in its place).

Nudge advocates claim that these concerns are not important because nudges are avoidable. Because nudges do not foreclose any other choices that people might want to make, they argue, people are not forced or coerced into the option "encouraged" by the nudge. But this argument denies the very reason nudges are so effective: They leverage the same unconscious cognitive quirks that lead to bad decisions. In the example of retirement programs, nudge advocates claim that people are too susceptible to the default of nonenrollment, so they change the default to enrollment. They take advantage of the same status quo bias that steered people toward the old default to steer them toward the new one that they chose. But this bias is no less powerful once the default is changed: If people found it hard to resist the default before it was changed, they will find it hard to resist it afterward. The same logic applies to the cafeteria example: They cannot claim customers were less likely to choose the salad when it was hard to reach and then argue that they are "free" to choose the banana split when it's just as well hidden. Supporters of nudge cannot claim that people are inevitably swayed by choice architecture in the absence of nudges but have the perfectly rational capability to overcome the same thing in their presence.

Choice Is About Interests, Messy as They Are

This is where the overly simplistic conception of choice comes in. Advocates of nudges—as well as supporters of more coercive forms of paternalism who are motivated by similar behavioral concerns—base their recommendations on the presumption that individuals have very simple and general interests, such as health and wealth. They use these presumed, simple interests as the basis for judging people's choices as well as for implementing policies to make these choices better (in terms of the presumed interests).

Paternalists defend these presumed interests as being general enough to apply to everybody, and certainly, most people have some concern for their bodily and financial well-being. But the fact that these interests are so general is also a drawback because individuals have specific and varied health-related and financial goals. With respect to health, some people want to lose weight, while others want to gain muscle; some are trying to cut back on sugar, while others trim back on meat; some are managing diseases or conditions, while others are trying to get pregnant (or avoid it). In the area of personal finance, some people are trying to maximize savings for retirement, while others are trying to buy houses, support family or charities, or simply enjoy life in the here and now. General presumed interests in health or wealth cannot capture these nuanced goals of individuals, especially when they push people's choices in one specific direction within them, such as promoting retirement savings over other equally valid goals.[26]

This reliance on a single general interest can be traced to how economists think about choice. In the standard economic model of choice, *homo economicus* decides how to use his scarce resources (money and time) to satisfy as many of his preferences or desires as possible. In the usual classroom example, Stan has $100 to spend on various goods that have different prices, and he has to decide how to allocate his money between the two goods, depending on how much he likes various amounts of one versus the other, to get the most bang for his buck (or, in this case, a hundred of them). This model, often called *constrained preference satisfaction*, can be elaborated upon to include incomplete information and uncertainty, but generally, it assumes that people try to get as much as satisfaction as they can with the resources available to them. This notion of satisfaction, often worded in terms of "utility," is purposefully vague in order to accommodate each individual's unique preferences and goals.

So far, so good. But in practice, and especially when it comes to policymaking, this all-encompassing idea of utility is replaced by the focus of the particular policy effort, such as health, wealth, or whatever narrower measure of well-being the government is hoping to promote. To some extent, this is natural: If you are working in the Consumer Finance Protection Bureau, you are going to be concerned primarily with making sure consumers get the most from their saving and borrowing, but if you are working for the Federal Drug Administration, you will be more concerned with health outcomes and mortality rates. This does not change the fact, however, that policy decisions meant to steer individuals' decisions for one narrow reason may have an adverse effect on other aspects of their lives not accounted for by that particular agency: Health nudges do not normally account for effects on personal finances, and vice versa.

This is a problem because individuals do not make decisions in pursuit of very simple goals such as health and wealth (or even their personalized, narrower versions of them). Instead, they make decisions based on the entire breadth of their interests, which are multifaceted, complex, and subjective.[27] This concept of interests goes beyond even economists' open definition of utility, which respects the different preferences individuals may have and even acknowledges that their preferences may be altruistic in nature. Most of us want to see our loved ones be happy and successful in what they choose to do; we may want the same for other people in our community, country, or the entire world. In other words, we care most obviously about our own preferences, happiness, or well-being, but also the preferences, happiness, and well-being of others. To their credit, some economists incorporate such altruistic motivations into their models, but the general assumption remains that individuals maximize their own well-being, and when evidence arises that they do not, it is treated as "exceptional" behavior because it is not predicted by the standard model.[28]

However, interests are *multifaceted* in that they go beyond regard for utility or well-being, even that of other people, to encompass principles and ideals. For example, most people value their honesty or integrity, which leads them to forego certain acts, such as lying or cheating, to satisfy their preferences. An economist may say that people simply have a "preference" for honesty—or, more cynically, a preference to be *seen* as honest—but principles don't influence our choices in the same way that preferences do. Rather than balancing a preference for honesty with a preference for the gain one could get from being dishonest, people are more likely to consider their honesty as ruling out dishonest action together, regardless of what they could achieve from it. More generally, principles are qualitative concepts of right and wrong that are difficult to weigh or balance against quantitative concepts of good and bad or better and worse. Instead, they are often considered to be different stages of decision-making, in which a person first considers whether an action is ethical or permissible before determining if it will benefit herself (or others she cares about).

In the same way, we also make choices to promote broader societal ideals, regardless of how these pursuits affect our preferences or well-being. We see this in people who devote their lives, figuratively and sometimes literally, to fighting for equal rights, environmental protection, or the humane treatment of refugees. Devotion to a cause greater than yourself is widely cited as a component of a deeper sense of happiness or well-being, but few people who exemplify this would cite this "reward" as their motivation; rather, they want to help make the world a better place, which, like adherence to personal principles, is very difficult to account for in the standard economic model of decision-making.

If this weren't enough, interests are also *complex* because all the different aspects of our interests are combined in different ways in different situations. Remember our example of trying to choose where to eat lunch, which was based on various preferences. But suppose you're concerned about the various restaurants' records on environmental, labor, and gender issues, and the question becomes even more complicated. Sometimes, these social factors may be foremost on our minds, and other times, we may just be craving an incredible burger. Or maybe one restaurant is great on labor issues but poor on recycling, and another has the reverse record—how to choose? This highlights the difference between preferences, which are easier to convert into comparable numbers and "optimized" (as economists are experts at doing), and principles, which are qualitative and therefore not easily compared to preferences. Many times, principled considerations override preferences altogether: For example, some people would never compromise their support of LGBTQ issues for a great burger at a restaurant whose owners have the opposite public stance, no matter how much they were craving one, while others who regard themselves as LGBTQ supporters might be willing to make such a compromise, perhaps because the restaurant has a terrific environmental record (or just a really good burger).

The multifaceted and complex nature of each individual's interests makes them very difficult to use as a basis for policy, even if everyone had the same interests. Preferences, principles, and ideals combine in complicated and fluid ways that resist modeling or prediction. But it's the *subjective* aspect of interests that poses the largest problem for policy because it makes them impossible for anyone to know. Only individuals themselves can possibly know the various reasons they make certain decisions, not to mention how those reasons are compared to each other and weighted or ranked to result in a final decision. Our friends from earlier who ate the banana split and put off retirement savings could have done so for any number of reasons, just a few of which we listed without even scratching the surface. In fact, we ourselves are usually not conscious of all the different aspects of our interests in which we make any decision; as we said before, much of it is done intuitively with interests operating under the radar of consciousness (or in our "gut").[29] But we usually have at least a vague idea why we made a particular decision, which is exactly one vague idea more than an outside observer such as a scholar or policymaker has.

When scholars or policymakers presume interests on behalf of individuals and judge their decisions based on these imposed goals, they are denying the multifaceted and complex interests in which individuals make choices. However well-intentioned these external observers are—and I trust that most of them are, having met quite a few of them—they are nonetheless usurping the freedom of individuals to make decisions in their own interests. They are co-opting their decision-making powers through the use of subtle nudges that leverage the very cognitive biases and dysfunctions that motivated nudges in the first place. Advocates of nudge claim to be helping individuals make the decisions they would make if they were more rational, but there is no way to know what decisions individuals would have made "if only"—instead, they are steered into making the decisions the policymakers think they should make, based on their idea of what is good for individuals.[30]

What Happens When We Neglect Interests

Much has been written, by myself and others, about the implications of nudge for individuals' autonomy.[31] This is an important concern: To the extent that nudges steer choices away from those individuals would have made in their own interests and toward ones that policymakers think they should make, individuals have less control over the choices they make and, more generally, the paths they want to follow in their lives. Many of the choices that nudges affect are small ones, but a sequence of choices that seem minor and inconsequential when taken individually add up to a life. Nudges force "course corrections" in individuals' lives, and we can imagine that if enough decisions were affected by them, significant parts of a life could be controlled as much by anonymous policymakers as by individuals themselves.[32]

I want to generalize from this point here, broadening the perspective away from the manipulative effect of nudges in particular to focus on the general mind-set at its foundation. To do this, we will return to the work of psychologists and neuroscientists that ground the nudge approach and look at the picture they paint of individuals and their decision-making that ignores the complex, multifaceted, and subjective nature of interests and, as a result, questions our *cognitive competency* and erodes the status of individuals in society.

To start, behavioral economists (and economists in general) are not alone in neglecting to appreciate the multifaceted and complex nature of interests. Any approach to looking at decision-making in a scientific way, which relies primarily on observation for data and then draws inferences from it, has the same problem. Psychologists present subjects in a laboratory—or, when they are lucky, in a naturally occurring situation—with different stimuli, observe their behavioral responses, and then try explain the causal connection in the most straightforward way possible, but always within some framework of how they think of choice to begin with.

Neuroscientists do much the same thing but with a focus on the brain itself, such as when they track which areas of the brain light up in an fMRI machine under different conditions or stimuli and then draw inferences based on the functions of the affected areas—again, based on their preconceptions of how choice works.[33] Even the most heavily data-based scientific investigation starts with a theory that the data "fills in." In the case of choice, this initial framework is based explicitly on economic models; in fact, the field of *neuroeconomics* developed, in part, because neuroscientists found the basic economic model of decision-making a useful foundation for brain research.[34]

If scientists start with a theory that implies perfect rationality, however, they set themselves—or rather, *us*—up for failure. As we've seen, many of these experiments show that our processes of rational thought are not as rational as researchers thought, and from that, they conclude that human decision-making is flawed. The problem is that their preconceived notion of perfect rationality is inaccurate as a description of human decision-making and therefore an inappropriate benchmark against which we compare our actual choice processes. This is like assuming that dogs can fly and then declaring all dogs to be "flawed" because they can't. This position that human rationality could (or should) be perfect can be useful as a point for scientific investigation to begin with, a null hypothesis to be rejected in the face of evidence, but not a preexisting belief to be confirmed or defended, much less a goal to be sought. This attitude explains the pessimism reflected in every article that reports a new "flaw" discovered in our decision-making processes, as if we really thought human beings were perfectly rational all along. Even the designation of cognitive biases and heuristics as "flaws" is reflective of this: Something can only be designated a flaw if it prevents that thing from serving its "assigned" function, like a dog that cannot fly or a human being who, contrary to assumption, is not perfectly rational.

Philosophers have long known that human beings are far from perfectly rational. For example, Aristotle wrote about the weakness of will and temptation as aspects of human nature, advising the development of virtues such as temperance and practical wisdom to overcome them.[35] Immanuel Kant, a champion of the power of rationality, nonetheless acknowledged problems with real-world human thinking, and similar to Aristotle, he recommended perseverance and the maintenance of strength of character in the face of temptation.[36] These observations correspond to the models of dual-process thinking of psychologists and neuroscientists, such as

Kahneman's System 1 and System 2 thinking (or automatic and controlled processes); in this way, scientific thinking has confirmed what philosophers have said for hundreds or thousands of years and surprises us only because we adopted overly simplistic ideas about human rationality in the years between.

Some psychologists and behavioral economists deny that perfect rationality is or should be the ideal. Instead, they follow in the spirit of Herbert Simon and understand our various cognitive biases and dysfunctions as an integral part of an effective decision-making process for human beings in the real world. Working separately, both Nobel laureates economist Vernon Smith and psychologist Gerd Gigerenzer developed the concept of *ecological rationality*, which regards human beings' decision-making processes as successful adaptations to their lived environments, rather than idealistic conceptions of what those processes "should" look like in a realm of abstract theory disconnected from actual experience.[37] As Gigerenzer and behavioral economist (and jazz bass prodigy) Nathan Berg write, "When heuristics, or decision processes—or action rules—function well in particular classes of environments, then ecological rationality is achieved."[38] What Smith and Gigerenzer have in common is, while they offer ways for individuals to make better decisions in pursuit of their interests, they don't start with the assumption that rationality "would be" or "should be" perfect if not for the shortcomings we have as natural, evolved beings.

Before scientists—whether they be psychologists, behavioral economists, or neuroscientists—suggest an explanation for an observed response to changed stimuli, they should reconsider their preconceptions about how human decision-making processes work, specifically the wide range and complexity of interests that ground our decisions. As explained above, scientists often assume a version of the simple economic model of choice, a process of devoting scarce resources to achieve wants, goals, or "rewards," which themselves are assumed to be simple and often singular (such as food, happiness, or dopamine). In general, this is the scientific process at its finest, using Occam's razor to find the simplest explanation to observed phenomena that also stands up successfully to replication (that is, without being falsified by future observations or experiments). Scientists do this to avoid introducing arbitrary or *ad hoc* considerations into experiments that will distort the environment or introduce unnecessary complications.

However, as Albert Einstein is widely regarded as having said, scientific explanations "should be as simple as possible, but no simpler."[39] Deciding which factors to include in your model or experiment is a judgment call based on the contributions and validity of each element, considered against the complication it introduces. Accordingly, a very simple model of choice is fine as long as none of the elements of choice that it leaves out are crucial to explaining the results of an experiment. For example, when studying the effects of "fake news" on likely voters, eye color can easily be left out of the equation; there is no reason to believe that people's susceptibility to fake news is related to the color of their eyes. However, while eye color would not be worth including, income and education are more likely to be relevant, and leaving them out would risk skewing the results of the study, compromising its validity and therefore its value in terms of providing information and insight. If important factors are left out of a model, it will neither describe reality well nor enable scientists to use it to form accurate and valuable predictions about the future.

This is where scientists—and the readers, scholars, and policymakers who make up their audience—are poorly served by a simple model of choice that fails to recognize the multifaceted and complex nature of interests. If researchers assume that every choice individuals make is driven by a simple pursuit of a singular interest, they will fail to understand behavior that is driven by the myriad other aspects of human choice. If they do not appreciate that individuals' choices are driven by principles and ideals as well as the pursuit of wealth, happiness, and other goals, they will not have these possible explanations at hand to interpret their observations, and instead, they will rely on only the tools provided by the basic model they use. In effect, the reliance on an overly simplistic conception of choice puts blinders on researchers who cannot see possible explanations of human behavior that lie outside the narrowly defined model they begin with, as we see every time a study confirming human beings' altruistic and principled behavior is reported as "surprising."

What makes this even more dangerous is that to many people, science has an illusory gloss of objectivity over it. In the popular understanding, science is shorthand for "knowledge" rather than a path to finding knowledge, a road that carries us forward to a brighter and better future but with a surprising number of bumps and twists.[40] Most people do not see the process behind science, the dedicated and brilliant but very human scientists in charge of the process, and much less the assumptions that they start the process with. As with any human institution, there are rules and standard within the scientific community to minimize the costs of these imperfections, but these safeguards are imperfect as well. Because most of us do not see the human side of the scientific process, we are likely to take reports of "surprising" irrationality more seriously than we should, because of the automatic credibility we implicitly grant to reports of new scientific discoveries (and the little attention we pay to retractions). We are also more likely to accept policy recommendations based on science without questioning either the assumptions made in the scientific investigations themselves or the ethical judgment needed to bridge the gap between scientific findings (what we *can* do) and policy initiatives (what we *should* do), as we saw in our earlier discussion of the missing link between individuals' bad choices and government nudges to help them make better ones. If we were more aware of the imperfections in the processes of scientific discovery and government policymaking, our own imperfections might not seem so bad!

What This Says About Us

While this misunderstanding of the nature of choice and interests is a problem for scientific practice and government policy, for the purposes of this book, the most problematic aspect of it is the image of the individual it leaves us with. When scientists and policymakers start with an unrealistic picture of how rational we "should" be and then discover that, in fact, we are not, the result is a picture of individuals as integrally flawed or broken. However, as we know, most people never seriously thought of human beings as perfectly rational to begin with. Certainly, we all make bad decisions from time to time, some of us more often than others and each of us more often in some circumstances than others. But only *we*, the decision-makers who are in a better position than anybody else to know the interests in which we make decisions, can know when they are bad. Rather than appreciating that individuals have multifaceted and complex interests in which they make choices—choices that may not always appear prudent to outside observers with no knowledge of these interests—these observers assume individuals are trying to achieve one goal and failing at it. They judge people's choices by standards that have nothing to do with people's own goals, like criticizing the dog who cannot fly, and they take it upon themselves to take steps to change these choices, all for people's "own good" (despite what the people themselves might think).

Science can reveal valuable and fascinating information about the mechanics of how we make choices, but it cannot determine *why* we make them on the first place. It cannot tell us the interests we are trying to further by making them—only we can know those (and imperfectly at that). Psychologists, economists, and neuroscientists have all studied the formation of preferences that, in their models, lead to choices, but they do not know the interests that ground those preferences.[41] Researchers can observe changes in behavior or brain scans corresponding to changes in stimuli, but they cannot observe the causal link, which can only be inferred based on their preconception of the basic mechanisms at work in the mind or brain, which brings us back to the overly simplistic model of choice that denies the richness of actual human decision-making. Once again, because most people aren't aware of the preconceptions regarding choice that underlie these results, they too easily accept the pessimistic interpretation of these scientific results at face value.

The ultimate result of all of this is the devaluation of individuals' own choices and interests and, by extension, individuals themselves. By assuming an unrealistic, overly simplified idea of human decision-making processes, and then "discovering" that actual human choices do not match this model, the presuppositions held by researchers about the flawed nature of individuals' choice faculties are confirmed. In other words, they set up unreasonable expectations and then take the failure of these expectations to come true as evidence that they were right to doubt them to begin with. This then leads to policy prescriptions designed to help individuals make the decisions they would have made "if only" they were perfectly rational (which, by implication, the policymakers must be themselves) and acting in their true interests (which, by implication, policymakers know better than individuals do).

This picture is one of the individual human being as a broken machine, incompetent to act in its own (presumed) interests due to a flaw in its hardware or programming. Of course, actual machines, like objects or things in general, have no interests. Instead, they have a purpose or function assigned to them by a person, either the one who invented it or the one who uses it. For example, the designer of a chair probably focused on people's comfort while sitting, while the person who purchases it may use it as decoration or… um… a place to stack books. (Hypothetically, of course.) The purpose or function of the chair is not inherent in the chair itself, but rather in how a person uses it.

Individual persons, on the other hand, have their own interests, which are influenced by any number of factors including genetics, upbringing, culture, religion, family and friends, and choice. Many of these influences are subtle or unconscious, and their development may have been gradual, but no true interest that a person feels devoted to is simply "assigned" to her or him, but to some extent are endorsed by the person upon reflection regarding how well that interest reflects his or her core values and character. (To what extent a person does this reflects her degree of *authenticity*, which we will discuss in the next chapter.) But the simple models of choice relied on by researchers and policymakers *do* assign interests to individuals as if they were objects or machines and then judge their choices to be "wrong" when they fail to further the interests "assigned" to them by those who presume to know better.

Another implication of viewing individuals as flawed machines is the way they are treated, aside from the presumption of their interests. For this point, I rely once again on Immanuel Kant, who drew a stark distinction between how we may treat persons and things: While things may be used simply as means to an end, persons must always be treated as ends in themselves.[42] When researchers and policymakers influence people's choices in interests which are not their own, they use these individuals as means to further ends which are not their own, often without the permission or even the knowledge of the individuals being affected. The benevolence of these third parties is irrelevant; it does not matter if they are sincerely trying to help people make better decisions. Because they are necessarily imposing interests on individuals in order to manipulate their concerns, they are using those individuals merely as means to these chosen ends and not as valuable ends in themselves. The policymakers are deciding for what purpose people should be making choices and interfering with these choices if they are not "correct," never mind what the individuals themselves regard as their interests or choices toward them. As a result, they are not being treated as persons with dignity and autonomy, making choices in their own interests; they may not make these choices perfectly even by their own judgment, but this does not imply that they are flawed or broken as might be judged by outside observers with their own conceptions of the individual's interests.

Most important, even the most complex machines have straightforward programming and hardware that knowledgeable people can understand and fix when they fail to support the purpose for which they were designed or used. But as we have seen, actual human decision-making processes are neither straightforward nor simple, and despite researchers' presumptions, they do not follow the rules of elementary logic and rationality. As we have seen, our brains evolved to solve problems to promote survival and reproduction, and some of those evolved biases and heuristics do not serve us as well today as they did for our ancestors thousands of years ago. Modern researchers perform an invaluable service by exploring these "quirks" in decision-making processes, but they should not presume to know, with any degree of certainty, what human beings' ideal process of rational thought is—much less the interests in which we would implement it. But they do presume to know this, as if our "programming" were as knowable as that created by humans themselves. This presumption generates a self-fulfilling prophecy by establishing an impossible standard for rationality which real human beings will inevitably fail to meet, and also supports a distorted picture of individuals that diminishes their value and denies them the respect they are owed.

Conclusion

In this chapter, we surveyed several aspects of psychology, neurosciences, and economics that, while valuable in their own right, contribute to a decline in respect for the individual in society as a whole. To be clear, this is less a fault with the science itself and more a matter of how the scientific results are interpreted: specifically, in the context of a mistaken belief that human beings are, or should be, perfectly rational. Against this background, any scientific discovery or development that points out that we are not perfectly rational is taken as one more reason why our decision-making faculties are flawed and our cognitive competency is to be questioned.

Throughout this book, we will explore more dimensions and implications of this shifting attitude toward the value of individuals and their relationship to society. In the next chapter, we will see how trends toward quantification, seen in the growth of algorithms and Big Data in government, business, and our own lives, tend to change the way we see ourselves in the same way developments in psychology and neuroscience do. For example, population research simplifies each of us to what external observers regard as our shared and vague interests and other characteristics, and our uniqueness as individuals is obscured and eventually ignored. Individuals are treated as essentially similar, possessing the same core interests of wealth, health, and happiness, as defined by researchers and policymakers, and any deviation of individuals from this is assumed either to be irrelevant or to average out in the aggregate. We'll see some of this emerge in the next chapter, which deals with the trend toward increasing quantification of human lives, by which the individual is represented, not by his or her character traits or personality, but by raw data, easily aggregated and analyzed by computer programs that do not realize the uniqueness of the individual.

Notes

1. Thorstein Veblen, "Why Economics Is Not an Evolutionary Science," *Quarterly Journal of Economics* 12(1898): 373–397, at 389.
2. Herbert A. Simon, "A Behavioral Model of Rational Choice," *Quarterly Journal of Economics* 69(1955): 99–118.
3. Herbert A. Simon, "Rational Choice and the Structure of the Environment," *Psychological Review* 63(1956): 129–138. For more recent work in the same spirit, highlighting the difficulties of making good choices, see Barry Schwartz, *The Paradox of Choice: Why More Is Less* (New York: Harper, 2004), and Sheena Iyengar, *The Art of Choosing* (New York: Hachette, 2010).
4. There is a wealth of books introducing the novice to the basics of neuroscience; I would recommend the many works of Michael Gazzaniga, the most recently being the autobiographical *Tales from Both Sides of the Brain: A Life in Neuroscience* (New York: HarperCollins, 2015). If neurological disorders are more your cup of tea, I recommend Oliver Sacks' classic *The Man Who Mistook His Wife for a Hat: And Other Clinical Tales* (New York: Touchstone, 1998).
5. Most of this work is contained in the following volumes: Daniel Kahneman, Amos Tversky, and Paul Slovic (eds.), *Judgment under Uncertainty: Heuristics and Biases* (Cambridge: Cambridge University Press, 1982); Daniel Kahneman and Amos Tversky (eds.), *Choices, Values, and Frames* (Cambridge: Cambridge University Press, 2000), and Thomas Gilovich, Dale Griffin, and Daniel Kahneman (eds.), *Heuristics and Biases: The Psychology of Intuitive Judgment* (Cambridge: Cambridge University Press, 2002).
6. New research suggests this is more than an unconscious result, however; see Jeremy A. Frimer, Linda J. Skitka, and Matt Motyl, "Liberals and Conservatives Are Similarly Motivated to Avoid Exposure to One Another's Opinions," *Journal of Experimental Social Psychology* 72(2017): 1–12, and Russell Golman, David Hagmann and George Loewenstein, "Information Avoidance," *Journal of Economic Literature* 55(2017): 96–135.
7. Hugo Mercier and Dan Sperber, "Why Do Humans Reason? Arguments for an Argumentative Theory," *Behavioral and Brain Sciences* 34(2011): 57–74.
8. In the next chapter we'll talk about algorithms affect how that information is provided.
9. A fantastic popular treatment of the various biases and heuristics can be in Dan Ariely's now-classic *Predictably Irrational: The Hidden Forces That Shape Our Decisions* (New York: Harper Perennial, 2010); for a more

academic overview, see Erik Angner's *A Course in Behavioral Economics*, 2nd ed. (New York: Palgrave Macmillan, 2016).
10. This book is 100% fat-free and sugar-free.
11. Daniel Kahneman, *Thinking, Fast and Slow* (New York: Farrar, Straus and Giroux, 2011).
12. We can even use these cognitive quirks to our advantage, as explained by Dan Ariely in his follow-up titled *The Upside of Irrationality: The Unexpected Benefits of Defying Logic* (New York: Harper Perennial, 2011).
13. To be precise, there had long been a field called behavioral economics, but it was overtaken by this new approach. On the transition from the "old" behavioral economics (inspired by Simon's work) to the "new" behavioral economics (based on Kahneman and Tversky), see Esther-Mirjam Sent, "Behavioral Economics: How Psychology Made Its (Limited) Way Back into Economics," *History of Political Economy* 36(2004): 735–760.
14. There has been pushback against behavioral economics. Richard Posner, a leading figure in the economic approach to the law, argued that behavioral economics does not propose anything that could not already be accommodated in traditional economic models of choice ("Rational Choice, Behavioral Economics, and the Law," *Stanford Law Review* 50(1998): 1551–1575, at 1552). On this theme, see also Richard McKensie, *Predictably Rational? In Search of Defenses for Rational Behavior in Economics* (Dordrecht: Springer, 2010).
15. Douglas G. Whitman and Mario J. Rizzo, "The Problematic Welfare Standards of Behavioral Paternalism," *Review of Philosophy and Psychology* 6 (2015): 409–425, at 410.
16. Gerd Gigerenzer, "On the Supposed Evidence for Libertarian Paternalism," *Review of Philosophy and Psychology* 6(2015): 361–383, at 365. For more on the relationship between traditional and behavioral economics, particularly in their shared reliance on the theoretical core of constrained preference satisfaction, see Nathan Berg and Gerd Gigerenzer, "As-if Behavioral Economics: Neoclassical Economics in Disguise?" *History of Economic Ideas* 18(2010): 133–165.
17. Seminal work includes Christine Jolls, Cass Sunstein, and Richard Thaler, "A Behavioral Approach to Law and Economics," *Stanford Law Review* 50 (1998): 1471–1550; Russell B. Korobkin and Thomas S. Ulen, "Law and Behavioral Science: Removing the Rationality Assumption from Law and Economics," *California Law Review* 88(2000): 1051–1144; Colin Camerer, Samuel Issacharoff, George Loewenstein, Ted O'Donoghue, and Matthew Rabin, "Regulation for Conservatives: Behavioral Economics and the Case for 'Asymmetric Paternalism,'" *University of Pennsylvania Law Review* 151(2003): 1211–1254.

18. Richard H. Thaler and Cass R. Sunstein, *Nudge: Improving Decisions about Health, Wealth, and Happiness* (New Haven, CT: Yale University Press, 2008). This book was based on earlier academic work, especially Sunstein and Thaler, "Libertarian Paternalism Is Not an Oxymoron," *University of Chicago Law Review* 70(2001): 1159–1202, and Thaler and Sunstein, "Libertarian Paternalism," *American Economic Review Papers and Proceedings* 93(2003): 175–179.
19. Thaler and Sunstein, *Nudge*, Chap. 6.
20. Ibid., pp. 1–4.
21. The term "libertarian paternalism" is provocative and controversial, as is implicit in the title of Sunstein and Thaler's paper "Libertarian Paternalism Is Not an Oxymoron." On the term itself, see Daniel B. Klein, "Statist Quo Bias," *Econ Journal Watch* 1 (2004): 260–271; Gregory Mitchell, "Libertarian Paternalism Is an Oxymoron," *Northwestern University Law Review* 99 (2005): 1245–1277.
22. For instance, see the UK's "nudge unit," the Behavioral Insights Team (http://www.behaviouralinsights.co.uk/), and their head David Halperin's book *Inside the Nudge Unit: How Small Changes Can Make a Big Difference* (London: WH Allen, 2015). In 2014 President Barack Obama instituted a similar initiative in the US government, the Social and Behavioral Sciences Team (https://sbst.gov/).
23. Some of this material was discussed in more detail in my earlier book, *The Manipulation of Choice: Ethics and Libertarian Paternalism* (New York: Palgrave Macmillan, 2013).
24. See Oren Bar-Gill and Elizabeth Warren, "Making Credit Safer," *University of Pennsylvania Law Review* 157(2008): 1–101; Michael S. Barr, Sendhil Mullainathan, and Eldar Shafir, "Behaviorally Informed Financial Services Regulation," New American Foundation (2008), available at http://www.newamerica.net/files/naf_behavioral_v5.pdf. For a critical view of this along the lines of my argument here, see my paper "Nudging Debt: On the Ethics of Behavioral Paternalism in Personal Finance," forthcoming in *Journal of Financial Counseling and Planning*.
25. Camerer et al., "Regulation for Conservatives," p. 1212.
26. For more on this, see my discussion of Cass Sunstein's *Why Nudge? The Politics of Libertarian Paternalism* (New Haven: Yale University Press, 2014), and Sarah Conly's *Against Autonomy: Justifying Coercive Paternalism* (Cambridge: Cambridge University Press, 2013), in my chapter "The Crucial Importance of Interests in Libertarian Paternalism" in Klaus Mathis and Avishalom Tor (eds), *Nudging - Possibilities, Limitations and Applications in European Law and Economics* (New York: Springer, 2016), pp. 21–38.

27. Again, see my paper "Crucial Importance of Interests" for more on the nature of interests and their… well… crucial importance.
28. See, for example, Howard Margolis, *Selfishness, Altruism, and Rationality* (Chicago: University of Chicago Press, 1984) and Serge-Christophe Kolm's "Introduction to the Economics of Giving, Altruism and Reciprocity" in Serge-Christophe Kolm and Jean Mercier Ythier (eds), *Handbook of the Economics of Giving, Altruism and Reciprocity, Volume 1: Foundations* (North Holland: Elsevier, 2006), pp. 1–122.
29. On our difficulties with accurate self-knowledge, see Timothy D. Wilson, *Strangers to Ourselves: Discovering the Adaptive Unconscious* (Cambridge, MA: Harvard University Press, 2002); Valerie Tiberius, *The Reflective Life: Living Wisely with Our Limits* (Oxford: Oxford University Press, 2008), chapter 5; and Quassim Cassam, *Self-Knowledge for Humans* (Oxford: Oxford University Press, 2015).
30. Philosophers and economists often use the concept of *ideal* or *rational preferences* to represent what preferences a person would have if, in the words of Nobel-winning economist John Harsanyi, "he had all the relevant factual information, always reasoned with the greatest possible care, and were in a state of mind most conducive to rational choice" ("Morality and the Theory of Rational Behavior," reprinted in Amartya Sen and Bernard Williams (eds.), *Utilitarianism and Beyond* (Cambridge: Cambridge University Press, 1982), pp. 39–62, at p. 55). The problem with ideal preferences is that they represent a counterfactual, an exercise in imagining a world different from our own. Furthermore, they involve the same value judgments as in presuming interests; as economist Robert Sugden asks, "How, without making normative judgments, do we determine what counts as complete information, unlimited cognition, or complete willpower? Even if we can specify what it would mean to have these supernatural powers, how do we discover how some ordinary human being would act if he were somehow to acquire them?" ("Why Incoherent Preferences Do Not Justify Paternalism," *Constitutional Political Economy* 19(2008): 226–248, at p. 232).
31. For example, see my *The Manipulation of Choice*; Riccardo Rebonato, *Taking Liberties: A Critical Examination of Libertarian Paternalism* (New York: Palgrave Macmillan, 2012); and Gilles Saint-Paul, *The Tyranny of Utility: Behavioral Social Science and the Rise of Paternalism* (Princeton, NJ: Princeton University Press, 2011).
32. This is not to mention the deleterious effect of nudges on decision-making processes themselves, for at least two reasons: nudges absolve persons of responsibility for their actions and deny them of important feedback from making bad decisions, and many nudges reinforce our cognitive biases and dysfunctions rather than reducing their influence. For more, see Jonathan

Klick and Gregory Mitchell, "Government Regulation of Irrationality: Moral and Cognitive Hazards," *Minnesota Law Review* 90(2006): 1620–1663.
33. See Paul W. Glimcher and Ernst Fehr, "Introduction: A Brief History of Neuroeconomics," in *Neuroeconomics: Decision Making and the Brain*, 2nd ed. (Amsterdam: Elsevier, 2014), pp. xvii–xxviii, which cites a seminal paper that "argued quite explicitly for a normative utility-based analysis of choice behavior in monkeys" (p. xxiv, citing M.L. Platt and Paul W. Glimcher, "Neural Correlates of Decision Variables in Parietal Cortex," *Nature*, 400(1999): 233–238).
34. See Glimcher and Fehr, "Introduction: A Brief History of Neuroeconomics," as well as Colin Camerer, George Loewenstein, and Drazen Prelec, "Neuroeconomics: How Neuroscience Can Inform Economics," *Journal of Economic Literature* 43(2005): 9–64. Both pieces give substantial background into basic cognitive neuroscience as well as the various ways it has informed economics (and vice versa).
35. See Aristotle, *Nicomachean Ethics*, 350 BCE, translated by W.D. Ross, Book VII (available at the Internet Classics Archive, http://classics.mit.edu/Aristotle/nicomachaen.7.vii.html).
36. See Immanuel Kant, *The Metaphysics of Morals*, translated and edited by Mary J. Gregor (Cambridge: Cambridge University Press, 1797/1996), pp. 408–409; see also my *Kantian Ethics and Economics: Autonomy, Dignity, and Character* (Stanford: Stanford University Press, 2011), pp. 57–59.
37. Vernon L. Smith, *Rationality in Economics: Constructivist and Ecological Forms* (Cambridge: Cambridge University Press, 1999); Gerd Gigerenzer, *Rationality for Mortals: How People Cope with Uncertainty* (Oxford: Oxford University Press, 2010).
38. Berg and Gigerenzer, "As-if Behavioral Economics," 21.
39. See this post at the Quote Investigator regarded the origin of this quote: http://quoteinvestigator.com/2011/05/13/einstein-simple/. A longer passage that does apply specifically to scientific theory appears in his 1933 Herbert Spencer Lecture: "It can scarcely be denied that the supreme goal of all theory is to make the irreducible basic elements as simple and as few as possible without having to surrender the adequate representation of a single datum of experience" ("On the Method of Theoretical Physics," *Philosophy of Science*, 1(1934): 163–169, at 165).
40. One terrific resource for explaining how science really works is "Understanding Science" (http://undsci.berkeley.edu/), a website produced by the Museum of Paleontology at the University of California at Berkeley.

41. For example, see Paul Slovic, "The Construction of Preference," *American Psychologist* 50(1995): 364–371; Amos Tversky and Richard Thaler, "Anomalies: Preference Reversals," *Journal of Economic Perspectives* 4 (1990): 201–211; Mkael Symmonds and Raymond J. Dolan, "The Neurobiology of Preferences," in Raymond J. Dolan and Tali Sharot, eds., *Neuroscience of Preference and Choice: Cognitive and Neural Mechanisms* (Amsterdam: Elsevier, 2012), pp. 3–31; and the chapters in Part II ("Neural and Psychological Foundations of Economic Preferences") of Glimcher and Fehr, *Neuroeconomics*.
42. See Kant, *Grounding for the Metaphysics of Morals*, translated by James W. Ellington (Indianapolis, IN: Hackett Publishing Company, 1785/1993), pp. 428–429. For more discussion of this essential Kantian concept, see Roger J. Sullivan, *Immanuel Kant's Moral Theory* (Cambridge: Cambridge University Press, 1989), pp. 195–198. Some astute readers may recognize this wording from Kant's famous—or infamous—categorical imperative, which we'll encounter later in this book. (I promise!)

CHAPTER 3

Big Data, Algorithms, and Quantification

The world is abuzz about data. We have information about everything at our fingertips, and we love it. It gives us a sense that we know more about ourselves: our fitness level, our diet, our energy usage, our productivity, and more. Others have data about us as well: Facebook, Google, and most other websites collect data on our browsing and purchasing habits, and they use this information in various ways to alter our online experience, boost their own profits, and potentially even influence elections. Finally, the government collects data on us as well, some benign (such as for tax purposes) and some less so (such as cell phone surveillance and public cameras with facial recognition capabilities).

This pervasive data collection brings up many issues, such as the nature of privacy and ownership of personal information, but the aspect I'll focus on in this chapter is the broader question about our embrace of *quantification*, which reduces our lives to 0s and 1s, and what that means about how businesses and the government see us and, perhaps more importantly, how we see ourselves.

There are several dangers in embracing "the quantified self" in our personal lives. For one, it can cause us to focus on those aspects of life that are easily counted or measured, such as steps, calories, words written, books read, miles runs or biked, or work performed, to the exclusion of deeper aspects of life, such as happiness, joy, respect, purpose, meaning, and connections to other people. It reduces more and more of life's experiences to numbers and in the process reduces life to those parts of it that can be quantified. In the worst-case scenario, we start to see ourselves as machines to be tracked and calibrated rather than complex human individuals with hopes, dreams, and passions, and this can have an effect on how we think of success and the good life.

While the personal dangers of excessive quantification may be a long way off, we are already seeing the dangers in terms of policy. More and more we are seeing that "Big Data" has an increasing influence on our lives, usually as processed through algorithms that are supposed to find scientific, objective answers to problems (including the problem of faulty decision-making discussed in the last chapter). These algorithms are to some extent present in personal tracking devices as well, although they are more self-directed—that is, the user is able to program the device according to the parameters she chooses. But the algorithms used in policy are designed and programmed by other people, and even if these people have beneficent goals, they are still, as in the case of nudges, acting in interests that are not necessarily in line with those of individuals. The popular understanding is that algorithms are scientific, objective, and therefore unquestionable, while in truth algorithms represent judgment calls made by the designer or programmer that guide how the bulk data is processed to arrive at particular decisions.

Furthermore, the reduction of the individual to data makes it even easier to ignore the unique nature, value, and dignity of the individual, and simply lump her into an aggregate which then can be optimized to achieve some larger goal (the "greater good"). We see this in the global trend toward "happiness policy," in which individuals' personal understandings of happiness and fulfillment are ignored in favor of a general or generic definition, against which people are assessed, and then the aggregate is used as the basis for policy. While this may sound better than simple economic aggregates such as output or income, this has the effect of eliminating the unique nature of the individual from the equation and reconceptualizing her as a mere piece of the puzzle, a contributor to the whole that then takes prominence and precedence. In general, this leads us to think of people as interchangeable, which is another step on the road to a utilitarian mind-set that diminishes the individual in favor of the collective and denies the essential rights we all value as human beings.

Numbers, Numbers Everywhere...

I'm from a generation that was fortunate to have come to age before the dawn of the Internet. I was able to watch it develop in size and scope with incredible speed, yet still be young enough to embrace it fully after it "matured." I remember big, clunky, standard-issue black rotary dial phones, when dialing a 9 or 0 was such a pain, and I love my shiny new Android cell phone today. I remember having the full set of Encyclopedia Britannica at home, which contained a small fraction of the information I can access instantly from that Android phone. I also remember having to see a movie in the theater, and if you missed it, you would hope it would come to television on one of the three networks. VCRs and VHS tapes came along soon, but those were nothing compared to the picture quality, instant access, and convenience of DVDs and Blu-ray Discs, which themselves were eclipsed by streaming services such as Netflix, Amazon Prime, and On Demand. (And don't even get me started on music...)

One of the aspects of technology that lies beneath all of these developments is the ability to store and process information cheaply and quickly. My first computer, an Atari 800, came with 16K of RAM—roughly speaking, 16000 bytes (8-bit chunks) of data. My dad spent $200 (in 1980 dollars, mind you) for an extra 32K of RAM to expand the computer to its *maximum operating capacity* of 48K. Ten years later, my first 16-bit PC (no Windows yet, just MS-DOS) contained 15MB of RAM—about 15 million bytes (16 bits each). As extravagant as this seemed to a young college student at the time, it is minuscule compared to the hundreds of gigabytes (billions of bytes of 64 bits each) common on desktop and laptop computers today. Even cell phones today can hold several gigabytes of data, and much more with just a tiny expansion card the size of your fingernail.

As the value, size, and availability of data storage have exploded over the years, so has the power of computers to process it. Tasks that would take room-sized computer days to perform several decades ago now can be done by a laptop in a few seconds. The smartphones we now use to send poop emojis to each other are many times more powerful than the computers that put Neil Armstrong on the moon in 1969.[1] (The Apollo Guidance Computer on the spacecraft itself had 64K of memory, not much more than my Atari 800.) If you consider all that our handheld devices can do, it boggles the mind to imagine what tasks a modern supercomputer can do—which does not even come close to the promise of quantum computing in the near future (perhaps by the time you are reading this book, or at least watching the movie version).

One way that we have put this plentiful data storage and processing capacity to use is in tracking and analyzing our own lives, in what has come to be known as "the quantified self" (a term popularized by *Wired* editor Gary Wolf).[2] Businesses and government have also embraced the new potential for mass data processing, or "Big Data," in ways that make services better and more customized, but also in ways that serve their own interests (which, to be fair, are valid as well and often coincide with our own). These uses may seem like a trivial application of computing power when compared to conducting lifesaving medical research, predicting the occurrence and impact of natural disasters, or exploring the origins of the universe. I would argue, however, that it has had a significant impact on people's lives in general, as well as the way that society, ourselves included, sees the individual, contributing the problems introduced in the last chapter.

…But We Should Stop to Think

While tracking our own lives with apps and devices seems harmless—and it can be, if done properly—as with most things, there are concerns if taken too far. At its most basic, the process of quantifying our lives reduces real-world complexity to simple numbers, eliminating any details that do not fit into 0s and 1s. As we saw in the last chapter, one problem with the psychology and neuroscience of decision-making was that researchers can only make observations based on behavior and brain states and then make inferences about the process behind them. They cannot directly observe the process, nor can they observe the "why" behind choice, namely the interests on which our decisions are made. When we quantify aspects of our lives, we make this problem even worse by not even trying to understand anything about choices, simply measuring and recording results in numerical form, stripped of nuance and context, which we then use to make further decisions without necessarily realizing how hollow those numbers are and how much meaningful information they leave out.

There is a staggering amount of information in the world, even just in the context of one person's life, and some of that information overload can be managed by putting as much of it as possible in the form of numbers. After all, what could be clearer than numbers—they go up, they go down, or they stay the same. They seem objective, as in the saying "the numbers don't lie." But while numbers may give the impression of clarity, how we interpret or use them is a different matter altogether. Better information does not necessarily lead to better decisions, especially if that quantitative information ends up taking precedence over qualitative information which may be more important.

For example, many of us track our body weight, caloric intake, steps walked, or exercises performed. (I'm one of them, to be sure. And no, I'm not going to share.) This is fine if such information is incorporated into a decision-making process that also includes other, less quantifiable aspects of health, such as fatigue, aches, and pain, and simply how we feel day to day, as well as life in general. If your scale ticks up a pound or two, it may be that you slipped in your diet or exercise routine, which can serve as a useful reminder to get back to it. But in some cases, there may be other reasons, "excuses" in the positive sense of the word that means the weight gain may not be your fault, and may even be understandable in the larger context of your life. Most obviously, weight fluctuates: Bodies are complicated, as we are learning more and more every day, and they have their own mechanisms for regulating weight despite what we may do to try to change it.[3] Or, maybe we attended our sister's wedding the day before and indulged—not because we forgot our eating regimen but because we felt that celebrating and participating in our sister's joy were more important. Sticking to a data-based plan for eating and exercise can be helpful, but not if we elevate the numbers, and their implications about our health, above everything (and everyone) else in our lives.

In general, the problem is that the wealth of data and analysis at our fingertips tricks us into forgetting the other aspects of our lives that are not so easily summarized in numerical form. Quantification distorts our perceptions according to the information that is available and plentiful and, as a consequence, leads us to favor those aspects of life and society that can be easily quantified, measured, and processed. In turn, this makes us liable to neglect those aspects which cannot be so easily converted into this format. (Talk about a modern-day cognitive bias!)

In a larger sense, this influences the way we see the world and each other, luring us into a world where everything—and everyone—can be translated into numbers or metrics. As sociologist David Beer writes in his book *Metric Power*,

> we are created and recreated by metrics; we live through them, with them, and within them. Metrics facilitate the making and remaking of judgments

about us, the judgments we make of ourselves and the consequences of those judgments as they are felt and experienced in our lives.[4]

Due to our impulse to quantify everything, aspects of our lives such as productivity, finances, and nutrition receive too much emphasis relative to their importance in a broader view of life, while less measurable but (some would argue) more important things such as meaning, happiness, and health are ignored. With respect to tracking weight and other body metrics, Beer mentions the Apple Watch, which he sees as "emblematic of both our creeping connectivity and the extension of metric power into our lives."[5] Even worse, those more qualitative aspects of life are forced into a quantitative measure—what Luigi Doria calls "the calculation of the incalculable human"—that lends them the appearance of precision and objectivity while obscuring their qualitative depth.[6] For example, the rich and complex human phenomenon that is happiness is reduced to numbers by surveys that only scratch the surface and inevitably impose a researcher's idea of happiness on the survey respondents (or leave the definition so vague that no respondent's results cannot be usefully compared to any other's).[7]

This example draws from the realm of policy, which we will discuss more later, but we see this same effect in the case of personal data as well. As Albert Einstein is widely thought to have said, "not everything that matters can be measured, and not everything that can be measured matters."[8] For many of us, the obsession with personal tracking of fitness, diet, and productivity can transform these activities from rich parts of human life to matters of measurable achievement (and even worse, the matters we choose to pay attention to).[9] This summons the image of corporate "efficiency experts" with their stopwatches, measuring hourly output on a production line, more than the way human beings should enjoy their lives. (Of course, this *may* be the way some choose to enjoy their lives and more power to them—but for others of us, we may be lured into this mind-set by the availability of all this data and apps to process it for us.) As long as we take the information provided by our tracking programs in the broader context of our lives, they can contribute to achieving our goals and furthering our interests. The danger is in letting the results of quantification guide our decision-making to an excessive degree and nudging ourselves into focusing too much on those aspects of our lives that are easily put into numbers and not enough on those that cannot.

Do the Computers Know Better?

In the case of our personal lives, we can take advantage of the ease and availability of data collection and processing to make our lives better, assuming we take it all in the proper context. This is not so easy for us to do when this information is used by other parties, such as businesses and governments, and we have much less control over how the way they use this information affects our lives—if we are aware of it at all.

Even though both business and government have an enormous impact on individuals' lives, they play very different roles and have different motivations that lead to different concerns about this impact, especially in the context of collecting and using information about individuals as customers or citizens. Generally speaking, businesses use Big Data and algorithms to boost their own profits, which are the presumed interests of the business owners, while governments use them in the interests of the citizens, whether presumed by policymakers as in the last chapter or conveyed explicitly through the democratic process. (Individuals or agencies within the government may also use information to further their own interests as well, of course, but for our purposes, we can assume benevolent and responsible policymakers. Corruption is another matter altogether!)

Another important difference between business and government is that as influential as many large businesses are in our lives, they have no coercive power, unlike the laws, policies, and regulations issued by the government. As we will see later, this makes governmental use of individuals' data of special concern due to the state's ability to enforce actions it implements based on that information.

The potential for coercion is not the only reason we should be more concerned when the government uses our data than when businesses do, even though businesses play a much larger role than the government does in the everyday lives of most people. Although it may seem counterintuitive, the fact that businesses collect and process our personal data for their own purposes is less of a concern than when the government does the same "for our own good." As we saw in the last chapter, even the most well-intentioned policy actions by the government in individuals' interests are misguided because they have no idea what those interests are. But businesses don't care what individuals' interests are, *except* insofar as that knowledge benefits them by enabling them to provide goods and services we are willing to spend money on and therefore make profit for them. When Amazon recommends another book to buy or Netflix recommends another movie or TV show for you to watch, they are trying to make another sale or keep a subscribing customer. They are using your previous buying or watching behavior to recommend other products you might be interested in—not for your own sake, ultimately, but for their own.

"Isn't this bad?", you might ask. Not at all: Just as you and I have our own interests, Amazon and Netflix have theirs. But their success at pursuing their interests depends on making us, their customers, happy (or, at least, satisfied with our purchases). They don't care if we're actually happy, and there is no reason they should—it's their own interest that leads them to act *as if* they care about ours. But they maintain no pretense that they "know" what's in our interests or that they are motivated to act in our interests; we know what they're after, and to the extent they're successful, it serves our interests as well. Commerce is not a zero-sum game in which one side wins at the expense of the other side losing. As any ECON 101 student knows, voluntary transactions increase value by allowing both sides to further their own interests by trading things with less value to them for things with more. That is the insight of Adam Smith's "invisible hand": In the area of lawful commerce, we can advance our own interests only by advancing others, by offering a good or service that other people are willing to pay us for, making both better off.[10]

The danger in these situations comes less from business using our data for their own good and more from the way we let them do it, as well as how we use the information they give us back. Just as we are lulled into a distorted view of our own lives by the amount of personal data at our fingertips, we can all too easily fall into the trap of letting businesses choose our purchases for us based on our analysis of our past behavior. Many people marvel at the accuracy of Netflix and Amazon's predictions, reporting that they choose our same movie or book for us that we would have chosen ourselves. To some extent, this is no surprise: Certainly, if you read one book by John Grisham, or one movie adapted from his books, they will probably recommend others by him, which you may very have chosen on your own.

This is natural, and what any stranger at a party might do if you mention the last book or movie you enjoyed, even without the benefit of complex algorithms and your complete purchasing history. Just like the stranger you chat with at the bean dip, though, Netflix and Amazon do not know if you have read or seen these recommended selections already—unless you purchased them through their services—much less if you even liked the one you just read or saw! These predictions are just that, informed guesses made by observing the patterns of behavior they have a record of and extrapolating them into the future. The more data they have, the better their predictions may be, and sometimes, they will get it right. But just as psychologists and neurosciences can see only the result of choices and not the reasons, patterns of past behavior only reveal so much to businesses, and none of them can know our future choices without knowing the complex and multifaceted interests that underlie them.

Similar to issues with our own uses of personal data, the algorithmic predictions of businesses can become problematic if we let them have too much influence on our choices without due reflection on their validity and foundations, as well as the larger context in which we make choices. This is not to say we should never consider or accept Amazon's book recommendations; sometimes, accepting the "advice" of business is completely reasonable. Certainly, if you're just mindlessly watching Netflix for the evening—perhaps just looking forward to the "and chill" part—you might just let it play one show after another, generally satisfied with its choices, but this is because you really don't care too much what you watch. But if you're actively watching, you want to choose your next show or movie, and for all of Netflix's data and algorithms, you know better than they do what you want to watch next, and in these cases, you should dismiss their recommendations. Many of us do, of course, but my concern lies with those who do not, those who sacrifice even that tiny bit of their own decision-making autonomy to other decision-makers they assume know better (with broader implications for our personal authenticity as well, as we will see later).

There are some who argue that ceding choices is a good thing, within limits. Cass Sunstein, whom we met in the last chapter as one of the authors of *Nudge*, more recently wrote a book titled *Choosing Not to Choose*, in which he argues for allowing others to make choices for you, at least in certain situations.[11] Sunstein writes that given the mass of decisions we make every day, and the limited cognitive and attentional capacity highlighted by psychologists and neuroscientists (as we saw in the last chapter), it isn't worth it for us to deliberate over every decision. Of course, we do not think about all of our choices; many of them are routine and automatic, as we spelled out at the beginning of the last chapter. But Sunstein argues that others, such as which book to order next from Amazon, may be worth "delegating" to other parties, such as businesses or government (similar to nudges, which rely on the same basic idea). If we feel that Amazon or Netflix makes the choices we would have made anyway, then following their lead would save us cognitive resources we can put to better use elsewhere in choice situations with more impact on our lives (and perhaps the lives of others).

Again, this is not controversial *per se*. There is no danger in following a recommendation once in a while, just as we might do when a friend tells us "oh you would love this movie, I thought of you when I saw it." Nor is this new: We already mentioned when it is reasonable to let Netflix show it what it "wants," and those of us old enough to remember listening to the radio to hear most of our music ceded our choices to the DJ—or, nowadays, a computerized programmer using listener data and algorithms to choose the playlist. The danger comes when we start following other people's (or businesses' or government's) recommendations automatically, letting their choices steer our lives. As a group of scientists writing in *Scientific American* agree, "often the recommendations we are offered fit so well that the resulting decisions feel as if they were our own, even though they are actually not our decisions. In fact, we are being remotely controlled ever more successfully in this manner. The more is known about us, the less likely our choices are to be free and not predetermined by others."[12]

If we are ceding choices consciously in order to devote our attention to more important tasks, in the active sense of "*choosing* not to choose," that is fine. But if we are doing it because we believe other people know us better than we do, that is a problem, because we are giving up control over our own lives, even in areas that seem trivial. This may make us more complacent when it comes to larger issues, such as accepting or ignoring politicians' controversial decisions out of misguided faith that they know what is best for us. As we will discuss later, this unreflective acceptance of the choices of others has serious implications regarding our own authenticity as individuals who determine our own choices according to our own interests.

CONTROL THE NEWSFEED, CONTROL THE WORLD

An area in which this reliance on the choices of others is especially dangerous deals with how we get our information about the world. There is an increasing concern about the role that algorithms play at companies such as Google and Facebook, which many of us use to find or receive information on a daily basis. More information should, ideally, contribute to better choices made in our own interests; using Internet services to get more information is, in this sense, the opposite of passively accepting others' choices. The irony is that in trying to make more informed, deliberate choices, we're getting information that was chosen and presented to us by other parties, usually on the basis of algorithms designed for purposes other than delivering the most objective, relevant, and timely information.

This danger was highlighted during the 2016 presidential election, when the scourge of "fake news" stories and manipulated newsfeeds were blamed for contributing to a campaign that was heavy on emotions and light on facts. Most of the criticism has been lobbied at the services filtering and distorting the information people receive—and these are certainly valid criticisms.[13] But I want to emphasize our uncritical acceptance of this information as fair, balanced, or accurate, despite our full knowledge that the companies providing this information are not acting in the public interest, much less our own.

If we apply the same market-oriented logic as above, we could argue that even though these companies are acting in their own interests, they are led to provide accurate and unfiltered information because that is what the consumers of information want; if they fail to do this, they will lose customers to companies that will do a better job. Back in the old days of print, everyone knew not to read the supermarket tabloids for serious news—you read *The New York Times*, *The Wall Street Journal*, or your local newspaper for that. But that was an easy distinction to draw: The *Times* and the *Journal* never had George Clooney's three-headed love child with a Martian on the cover. It is more difficult to look at the results of a Google search, or the newsfeed on a Facebook or Twitter page, and decide whether it is an accurate and unbalanced reporting of the day's news. We would need additional information to do that, but it is difficult to be sure the source of that information is unbiased; even "media watchdog" and fact-checking sites have their own points of view. (The cautionary question *quis custodiet ipsos custodes?*, or "who watches the watchmen?", applies well here.)

This problem makes it much more difficult for people to switch from less accurate to more accurate sources of information and thereby removes this essential market discipline from the media industry. Without that discipline, information providers are not led by the invisible hand to provide quality information in order to keep customers; as long as customers are satisfied with the information they receive, the companies will not change. As a result, companies can provide the information they want to provide, how they want to provide it, and trust that consumers will accept it regardless of any lack of bias or objectivity.[14]

This is hardly a fanciful prediction; we see it already. For example, people have started questioning whether Google and Facebook could manipulate (or have manipulated) information feeds for political reasons.[15] Many of us are complicit in this as well, especially those of us who get our news from sources that verify our preexisting beliefs—an example of the confirmation bias we discussed in the last chapter, but deliberately embraced rather than unconscious. Liberals and conservatives have long read different newspapers and magazines and watched different cable news channels, and now, they follow different news sites, blogs, and Twitter feeds, resulting in the ideological "echo chambers" written about so much since the 2016 election (although they existed much earlier).[16] To some extent, this is a conscious choice to read or hear viewpoints that individuals agree with and to block out those they do not. But within these choices, people are ceding the information they receive to what these providers choose to give them; if this is taken too far, as George Dyson wrote, "Facebook defines who we are, Amazon defines what we want, and Google defines what we think."[17] We must always remember that while we may be choosing who curates our information, they're still the ones doing the curating.

Algorithm, Al Got Music...

This highlights another important aspect of quantification and Big Data that often gets overlooked: the algorithms that process the data into information so it can be used to make choices, regardless of by whom (or for whom). Data is useless by itself; to paraphrase Carl Sagan, data alone is billions and billions of numbers which mean nothing without interpretation within a certain context, which can be provided within a complex computer formula or an old-fashioned human process of aggregation, selection, and curation. Even Nate Silver, modern wizard of statistical prediction—the 2016 presidential election aside—confirms that "numbers have no way of speaking for themselves. ... Data-driven predictions can succeed—and they can fail. It is when we deny our role in the process that the odds of failure rise."[18] Websites such as *Vox* and Silver's *FiveThirtyEight* are not simply throwing numbers at you and asking you to make sense of them; they are making sense of them in some way, adding context and background that they have chosen. It would be naïve to argue that their own presumptions and viewpoints do not influence the way the data is presented and interpreted; the best they can do is be transparent about how they make these choices.[19]

There are many examples of this, and it's a phenomenon that has gotten much attention in recent years. It's no secret—and is in fact part of their business plan—that Google's search algorithm favors websites that have paid them for premium placement in search results. We have already seen the potential for information aggregators such as Facebook to manipulate the presentation of news for political purposes. But this is not necessarily an indictment of these websites and the people who run them and design the algorithms. Algorithms have to be designed somehow and with some goal or purpose in mind. The problem with the examples above is that they were designed for purposes that do not align with the interests of most of their end users who count on them for some degree of impartiality or objectivity in online searches or newsfeeds.

The most important point to recognize is that algorithms are not handed down from above, but are designed by human beings with their own goals, interests, and flaws. As mathematician Cathy O'Neil writes in her book *Weapons of Math Destruction*, "many of these models encoded human prejudice, misunderstanding, and bias into the software systems that increasingly managed our lives," whether through the design of the algorithms themselves or through the choice of the data the algorithms would process.[20] This fact is easy to forget because the word "algorithm" sounds so technical, "math-y," and scientific. Even when we do acknowledge that human beings are behind their design, we usually picture bespectacled secular monks, dedicated computer engineers who design algorithms for an obvious, clear, and noble purpose as pristine and pure as their white laboratory coats. We don't like to think of a team of marketers, financiers, and political activists looking over the programmers' shoulders and tweaking the algorithms to provide results that are in the interests of the company or its owners rather than the customers.

We saw this illusion of objectivity in the last chapter in the case of psychological and neuroscientific results being used to guide behavioral policy, which gives the impression that the policy itself is scientific. There is an essentially human component that translates science into policy, an intermediate step that involves judgment and choice, not simply deductions from scientific principles. The same thing occurs with Big Data and algorithms, both in the collection of the data itself—determining which data is collected for whom and how—and in the processing of the data.

This has been widely recognized by scholars in the humanities. Historian Theodore Porter describes quantification as a "technology of distance," a distance that is supposed to lead to objectivity, that "implies nothing about truth to nature" but rather "the exclusion of judgment, the struggle against subjectivity," which in the end is an illusion because all data is generated and processed using human judgment and subjective values.[21] Beer writes that "numbers seem to place their users at critical and objective distance from the object that is being judged and the decision that is then being made. If calculation provides a sense of distance, then quantification is providing the opportunity to judge value at a distance and to make such judgments appear hyper-rational, fair, and indisputably logical."[22] As political economist Will Davies writes, this line of thinking seeks "to replace critique with technique, judgment with measurement," but this all depends on earlier decisions "about *what* ought to be measured, and *how* it is legitimate to represent this objectively."[23] These earlier decisions happen before later choices are made based on the numbers, choices which again depend on human judgment, rather than flowing directly and logically from information itself. In reality, it is judgment all the way down: The data may be simply numbers, but how they are generated, processed, and implemented is all due to human beings using their judgment to make choices.

Even if these algorithms were designed to further the interests of the final users, the criticisms that applied to behavioral policy are still relevant. To the extent that these institutions claim the algorithms are designed to promote the interests of individuals—even if this is their sincere intention—the algorithms, no matter how complex, cannot replicate the process of decision-making and judgment employed by a single individual, much less millions of them. The same simplistic conception of decision-making that underlies behavioral science and policy is also at the heart of algorithms designed to analyze and predict our behavioral patterns. To be fair, they cannot do any better: As we saw, the multifaceted, complex, and subjective nature of interests makes it impossible to incorporate them into any precise model, and we do not know enough about the actual how and why of human decision-making to incorporate a realistic picture into algorithms, especially with all the quirks and "imperfections" chronicled by psychologists and neuroscientists. We can acknowledge and consider the recommendations of algorithms, but we should acknowledge and remain aware of this inability of algorithms (or their programmers) to know our true interests and resist putting too much faith in algorithms to anticipate our future decisions.

Does this mean any attempt to understand and predict human decision-making is doomed to failure? Not necessarily—it all depends on how we define failure. Any reasonably accurate information can be useful; the important thing to remember is not to put more weight on a certain bit of information than it deserves and keep it in the proper context. For example, the confidence intervals reported with political polling results give important signals about how precise they are. The qualification of "+/- 5 points" is an explicit recognition of the statistical inaccuracy of those results. The more people the pollsters survey, the more accurate the resulting information will be, and the tighter the confidence interval they can report (plus or minus three percentage points rather five, for example). But we do not usually get confidence intervals for the results of algorithmic analysis of Big Data, so it carries the imprimatur of precise and objective science. As we saw in the last chapter, this leads us to put more trust in, or weight on, these results, much more than they might deserve if we were fully aware of the source of the raw data and the design of the algorithm processing it.

By the same principle, if the information resulting from such analysis were simply being reported in a human-interest story in a newspaper or magazine, it would be entertaining but harmless. To the extent this information is being used to make decisions, however—whether personal ones regarding diet, exercise, or purchases, business ones regarding product launches, promotion strategies, or price schedules, or government policy regarding budgeting priorities, criminal justice, or homeland security—the inaccuracy and imprecision of the information, as well as the way in which it was generated, are of tremendous importance, especially in the context of government policy that has the coercive power of the state behind it.

Just the Data, Ma'am

As concerned as we should be about business and its use of personal data—and how we, in turn, use their recommendations based on it—we should be concerned for different reasons about the government's use of Big Data and algorithms to make legal and policy decisions, considering the aspect of coercion implicit in law and policy, as well as the presumptive nature of even the most well-intentioned governmental decisions regarding personal behavior. More generally, however, we see the same themes of the "obvious" and scientific nature of governance based on Big Data and algorithms, stemming from the mistaken understanding that they are objective, rational, and unquestionable.

The most obvious and pernicious example is the use of data obtained by surveillance, whether electronic or otherwise. At risk of sounding like John Malkovich's character in the *RED* movies—an exemplar of paranoia if there ever was one—our governments collect more and more data about us than ever before, from the increasing number of cameras everywhere, tracking of our cell phone and browsing data, monitoring of e-mail, and the maintenance of financial records (which has actually been used as an argument for a cashless society, because cash transactions leave no trail).[24] The same availability of data storage and processing capacity that allows Amazon to predict our next purchase and Google to cater our searches to our online personalities also leads the way to a brave new world in which the government can conduct policy in a much more effective and individualized way—for better or for worse.[25]

Of course, no one wants the government to do the business of government without the information it needs (whatever the scale and scope of government you happen to favor). In order to conduct economic policy, various government agencies collect data on output, employment, and prices; to conduct criminal investigations, detectives gather clues and interview witnesses and "parties of interest." But in these cases, both the way data is collected and the way it's used and processed are fairly transparent. In contrast, the use of Big Data in so many aspects of our lives, and the process by which mysterious, "black box" algorithms (in the language of legal scholar Frank Pasquale) surreptitiously turn this data into actionable information, make this aspect of government activity mysterious and unaccountable.[26] The fact that algorithms are falsely regarded as objective, scientific, and nonpolitical grants government agents more discretion to use them as they choose. As Pasquale writes, "technocrats and managers cloak contestable value judgments in the garb of 'science,'" leading to "the insatiable demand for mathematical models that reframe subtle and subjective conclusions (such as the worth of a worker, service, article, or product) as the inevitable dictate of salient, measurable data."[27]

Furthermore, because they always have the stamp of approval from science to back them up, policymakers can claim that they are just doing what the data "tells them" needs to be done. As Beer writes, "data is simply seen to be better than anything any human intuition or judgment might offer. The data says this—that is the end of the story."[28] This can have extremely dire implications; philosopher Hannah Arendt delivered a scathing indictment of decision-making during the Vietnam War when she wrote "the problem-solvers did not *judge*; they calculated."[29] What is more, it is difficult to argue with the data because of this apparent obviousness; numbers "are simply too weighty and convincing to simply be dismissed or undermined," which is "the problem for those wishing to resist their logic," who often have "only" anecdotal evidence, not "hard numbers," to back their case.[30] But as we said earlier, there is always human judgment involved in translating information into action, whether that judgment is embedded in algorithms themselves or invoked when the information supplied by algorithms is put to use. Data and information do not lead to political action unless some human being programmed it to do so or chooses to use it that way. Much like how our creation and use of personal data shape the way we see ourselves, "how such numerical assessments are created, produced, cast into the world, and used has significant implications for the way the world is understood and governed."[31]

As an example of how Big Data and algorithms have affected governance, we can look at criminal justice. Law enforcement agencies have turned to Big Data and algorithms to direct resources to areas with higher crime rates, often based on statistical analysis of a geographic breakdown of a city, with significant results.[32] Proponents argue that the reliance on "objective" statistics and computers is an improvement over human judgment that sometimes resulted in biased policing and racial profiling. The results of algorithmic policing often display the same patterns of bias and discrimination as traditional methods, however, illustrating the points made above that algorithms are not objective by nature, but often include human bias in their programming itself or in the way that their results are implemented. As Pasquale writes, "in contexts like policing, there is often no such thing as 'brute data,' objective measures of behavior divorced from social context or the biases of observers."[33] For example, the algorithm used to assign police officers to certain "high-risk" parts of town is often based on minor crimes such as vandalism and panhandling, which comprise the bulk of the arrests and confirm the area's "high-risk" status in what O'Neil calls a feedback loop, even if this judgment is not based on the major crimes the algorithms are meant to anticipate and prevent. Furthermore, due to the segregation in most of our major cities, "geography is a highly effective proxy for race," which creates a vicious cycle for impoverished minority neighborhoods. More recently, surveillance has been incorporated into predictive policing; as a result, it is not only areas and neighborhoods that are targeted, but individuals themselves, based on the data from facial recognition and social networks which have led police officers to tell individuals they are "being watched" before they break a single law.[34] (If you think this is reminiscent of the 2002 movie *Minority Report*, you would not be alone.)

Another example of criminal justice is the process of making sentencing decisions for convicted criminals based on algorithms designed to predict recidivism. These results have been shown to be biased against African Americans based on the types of questions asked, such as whether a person has had any prior interactions with the police or whether they know any criminals, which are more likely to be answered in the affirmative by those who have grown up in high-crime areas.[35] Furthermore, because an individual may be labeled as "high risk" by an algorithm, he or she will be given a longer sentence—based on a higher calculated risk of recidivism—exposing him or her to actual criminals for even longer and increasing the true chances of recidivism in a self-fulfilling prophecy (or feedback loop). This is not to deny the benefit of more information in the hands of law enforcement, but simply to point out that data and algorithms do not solve the problem of bias, but merely dress it up in a sheen of objectivity that can obscure the ever-present role of human judgment and error. This problem is made even worse by the secrecy of the algorithms' private owners regarding their trade secrets that prevent those sentenced from confronting their "accuser."[36]

Broadening the scope of Big Data and algorithmic governance, we find another example in the realm of "happiness policy." When tracking the well-being of their citizens for policy purposes, governments around the world in recent years have been shifting their emphasis from the narrow, economic measures of output or income to broader conceptions of happiness. Not only does the concept fall prey to the same problems of subjectivity that we saw in the last chapter, but it also highlights the issues with quantification discussed in this one. Put simply, happiness is far too vague and broad a concept to be defined precisely enough to be measured accurately enough to say anything meaningful about a population for the purpose of enacting policy.[37] The judgment of researchers and policymakers is embedded in the definitions they choose and the measurements they conduct; in the end, any reported results beg the question of what they were measuring in the first place, which is one specific conception of happiness, not what any one person surveyed thinks it is (much less every individual asked). Once again, the gloss of "science" is used to render a complex and personal notion such as happiness into data in order to convince people that the results are objective and undeniable, without revealing the many layers of human judgment behind the numbers and their policy implementation.

This impulse to convert what is essentially a qualitative human experience into cold numbers for the sake of measurement and manipulation is indicative of a larger drive within modern government and society as a whole. As economist Nicholas Eberstadt wrote in his book *The Tyranny of Numbers*, "the modern state is an edifice based on numbers," in which bureaucrats suffer from what sociologist Pitirim Sorokin called "quantophrenia," or an idolatry of numbers.[38] As I've tried to emphasize here, numbers, data, and algorithms are useful and to some extent unavoidable, but at the same time, they must be used and interpreted responsibly; as Eberstadt continues, "when all is said and done, there can be no substitute for moral reasoning in human affairs. The statistics-oriented, meliorative state may be new, but the question of how to use knowledge in a morally responsible manner is not."[39] The apparent objectivity and rationality that make numbers seem unquestionable must always be resisted as well. As anthropologist Sally Engle Merry writes in her book *The Seductions of Quantification*, "indicators are appealing because they claim to stand above politics, offering rational, technical knowledge that is disinterested and the product of expertise." Because of this, "statistical information can be used to legitimate political decisions as being scientific and evidence-based in time when politics is questioned. ... Such technocratic knowledge seems more reliable than political perspectives in generating solutions to problems, since it appears pragmatic and instrumental rather than ideological. These are the seductions of quantification."[40]

My purpose here is not only to critique the use of Big Data and algorithms by the government or business, which is one sign of declining respect for the individual in society, but also to explore why we're so willing to accept it. This is a sign of declining self-respect as individuals in the sense that we are too willing to cede our judgment to that of other parties. As with the psychology and neuroscience in the last chapter, we are too willing to trust that anything presented in scientific language or numerical form is objective and unquestionable. At the end of *The Seductions of Quantification*, Merry writes that "both in policy circles and in the general public, there is a faith that numbers and scores can provide secure knowledge of a world that seems unknowable," but while "quantification has a great deal to contribute... it is important to resist its seductive claim to truth and to recognize it as only one form of knowledge with its own distinctive limitations."[41] Porter summarizes this concern well when he writes, "quantification is a powerful agency of standardization because it imposes order on hazy thinking, but this depends on the license it provides to ignore or reconfigure much of what is difficult or obscure."[42]

The underlying science in all of these cases is valid and valuable, but we must remember that none of it can be interpreted or implemented without human judgment, which reflects values that must be examined and questioned to make sure they are consistent with values we maintain, either individually or as a society. As O'Neil writes, "Big Data processes codify the past. They do not invent the future. Doing that requires *moral imagination*, and that's something only humans can provide."[43] As always, the essential distinction is between what we *can* do and what we *should* do: Science continually expands the realm of what we're able to do, which places higher demands on us to decide what we should do with these expanded capabilities. We have a responsibility as individuals, consumers, and citizens to be mindful of these effects and to hold those in power accountable for the choices they make on our behalf. And most important, we need to maintain respect for ourselves as individuals by making our own choices in the face of influence from others, and even when we do accept this influence, we need to do so reflectively and consciously, not automatically and passively.

What This Means for Us

We have already seen how quantification, like the psychology and neuroscience discussed in the last chapter, minimizes and obscures the nuanced interests and judgment of individuals. Another danger, present in all of these cases but most clearly apparent with regard to quantification, is that the difference between individuals is blurred: Persons become indistinguishable, leading to a social and political focus on the whole instead of the parts that make it up. This aspect of the decline in respect for the individual will be a prominent theme in the rest of this book, and this final section of this chapter will provide a link between the more science-based discussions in these first two chapters and the more humanistic material to follow.

When the behavior, choices, and lives of human beings are reduced to numbers, this risks individuals themselves being regarded as directly comparable and, ultimately, exchangeable or substitutable. After all, numbers serve exactly this purpose: They allow amounts and quantities of things to be summed, compared, tracked, and manipulated. As long as the numbers based on individuals are taken in context and considered within the broader scope of life, they can be tremendously helpful, as I've tried to emphasize in this chapter. It is only when they're relied upon exclusively that there is a problem—and this problem becomes immeasurably more serious when numbers entirely take the place of the individuals whose lives they summarize (inaccurately and abstractly). If these numbers receive more emphasis than the human beings they describe, and researchers and policymakers get used to focusing and acting on those numbers without

3 BIG DATA, ALGORITHMS, AND QUANTIFICATION   59

mindful consideration of their source, the uniqueness and distinctiveness of individuals may be lost.

We can use an example from economics to illustrate this problem. Consider how the most widely used measure of national output, gross domestic product (GDP), is understood and calculated. The purpose of GDP is to account for all of the goods and services produced in a country in the span of a year. Technically, this wouldn't be a single number but rather a list of every single good or service made in the country and how many or much of it was produced. This would be complete and accurate, to be sure, but not very useful for tracking the size and growth of the economy over time, given the size and complexity of the list, which would have to include every variety of cheeseburger, lawn mower, and medical service produced or provided.

To make GDP useful, then, we need a way to summarize this list, collapsing it into a single measure of national output. How can we do this? It's literally a problem of apples and oranges—and the thousands upon thousands of other goods and services produced in even the smallest economy. We can't simply count up the output, for several obvious reasons. For one, some products, such as milk, are measured, while others, such as eggs, are counted. Also, our measure needs to reflect that a larger or more elaborate product should count as more output than a smaller or simpler one. An automobile represents more production than a bicycle, and the creation of a huge cross-platform advertising campaign represents more work than making an "everything 50% off" sign.

In other words, a measure of national output should reflect relative value between different goods and services as well as different varieties of each good and service. The easiest way to do both is to count each "bit" of output by its market price, which is strongly (if not perfectly) related to the amount of production or work that goes into it. This allows all goods and services sold in the market to be measured in a common unit—typically, the unit of currency in the country—that is easily available, and results in one number that can be compared to similarly computed numbers in other years and other countries (after adjusting for changes in the value of currency over time and between countries).

This is a reasonable way to derive a single measure of national output (if not well-being).[44] It works because things—goods and services—are inherently comparable, especially when there is a convenient common metric that can be used to value them all in the same units. Even as the mix of goods and products changes from year to year, we can still tell if the overall level of output has risen or fallen (again, after changes in the price level or value of the currency are taken into account). Because of this comparability, thousands or millions of widely different goods and services, including new ones that are introduced each year, can be included in one common measure. It is not a perfect measure, but it serves this particular purpose well and therefore has value as long as it's taken in the proper context.

As we saw in the last chapter, however, persons are not things, as emphasized by philosopher Immanuel Kant. Kant highlighted the exchangeability of things but not persons when he wrote, "whatever has a price can be replaced by something else as its equivalent . . . whatever is above all price, and therefore admits of no equivalent, has a dignity": namely, persons.[45] Things can be exchanged based on their relative worth, and even the abilities of a person can be priced according to their value to other persons (as in a wage–labor system). But persons themselves cannot be valued in such a way; they are literally priceless because their value (their dignity) is immeasurable and incomparable. This dignity grounds human rights that take precedence over collective welfare, as embodied in the Declaration of Independence (with its claim of the "unalienable rights" of all individuals) and the Bill of Rights to the US Constitution (stating that "Congress shall make no law" violating certain individual rights) as well as other documents around the world, such as the United Nations Declaration of Human Rights (which asserts the "inherent dignity" and "the equal and inalienable rights of all members of the human family").

By converting so much of human choice, behavior, and experience to numbers, the trend toward greater quantification threatens to render persons more like things in the eyes of government, business, and ourselves. Of course, no one is seriously advocating tallying up the value of human beings, although this attitude is implicit in the views of those who would deny certain persons any value whatsoever (or ascribe a lesser value to persons based on their gender, race or ethnicity, religion, or sexual orientation). Nonetheless, reducing so many aspects of our lives in the form of numbers lends persons the appearance of comparability—as Beer put it, these aspects must "similar enough to measure, but different enough to compare"—and thereby obscures our uniqueness.[46] As Merry writes, "counting things requires making them comparable, which means that they are inevitably stripped of their context, history, and meaning," and these aspects of human lives are too important to be neglected, ignored, or forgotten.[47]

Once information about people can be quantified and aggregated, the resulting total or average can be "adjusted" through policy, as is done with impersonal economic statistics like GDP, and increasingly, personal measures such as happiness. As many have noted, and in the words of Porter, "numbers turn people into objects to be manipulated."[48] No longer are the individual's characteristics taken seriously or respected, but instead, they are collapsed into the total, after which it is the total that gets the attention to the exclusion of the individuals that make it up. As geographer Stuart Elden wrote, "when humans are summed, aggregated and accounted for," then "much remains forgotten, unsaid, concealed," which makes it easier to take action that denies their rights, their interests, and their dignity as individuals.[49] As philosopher William Irwin put it very artfully, "the old saying has it that we can't see the forest for the trees, but the neglected problem when it comes to the individual and society is that we can't see the tree for the forest."[50]

A natural extension of the elimination of individuality caused by quantification and aggregation is *utilitarianism*, the approach to ethics that judges the morality of actions by their effect on total utility or well-being. When utilitarianism was first popularized in the eighteenth and nineteenth centuries by Jeremy Bentham and John Stuart Mill, it was revolutionary for the fact that it treated each individual's utility equally when adding up the total, regardless of a person's class, gender, race, or religion.[51] While this element of moral equality is admirable, it carries with it a disturbing aspect of equivalence in that it renders each person's utility substitutable or exchangeable for every other person's. Ultimately, it does not matter if a policy benefits Susan or Steve because an increase in either person's utility will increase the total. If the same policy can benefit either Susan by a certain amount or Steve by a greater amount, the policy should be focused on Steve because that would increase total utility by a greater amount, regardless of whether Steve is more deserving or has a greater claim on that benefit. Even more troubling, if a policy can increase Steve's utility by a certain amount only if Susan's is lowered by a smaller amount, a utilitarian approach would recommend that policy because it will increase the total, regarding the harm imposed on Susan, again with no consideration of desert. Individual identity does not matter because all persons contribute their well-being equally to the total, which is the only concern to a utilitarian policymaker.

The utility of individuals, although based on their unique interests, can be easily exchanged or traded for one another because it is all the same in terms of numbers, which take the place of the unique interests they are based on. As philosopher John Rawls wrote, by making the false analogy between an individual making the best choice for herself and society doing the same in terms of its "own" collective interests, utilitarianism "does not take seriously the distinction between persons," which is the objection we have seen many others make to the program of quantification as well.[52]

This is but one example of utilitarianism's implication that "the ends justify the means": that we should do anything it takes to increase total utility even it violates moral norms based on the dignity of persons and other considerations aside from utility. Philosophers talk about hypothetical scenarios in which a tyrannical dictator has the choice whether to kill one innocent protestor to calm a violent mob that may result in many more deaths, or the infamous "trolley problem" in which a person must decide whether to sacrifice one bystander to save five passengers on a runaway trolley car.[53] These are useful examples to ponder in the classroom, the seminar room, or the bar afterward, but their fictional nature tends to obscure the real-world effects of utilitarian decision-making, especially as it concerns the rights of individuals that are sacrificed to a vision of "the greater good." We will see more examples of this later, but any policy that benefits some persons while taking from others is based on this brand of logic—which does not make such policies wrong *per se*, but does require additional justification to explain why some persons should be forced to make sacrifices for the good of others.

Conclusion

We'll discuss utilitarianism and the individual much more in the rest of this book. In the meantime, however, we must always be careful to remember that even though we should be very critical of government policy that fails to respect the dignity of the individual, this state of affairs was not imposed on us by a tyrannical state. By the same token, the wealth of personal data collected and used by businesses was not entirely a usurpation of our lives by outside forces. To some extent, we accepted this new approach to policy and commerce. Our self-respect as individuals has been eroded by what we read and hear about new developments in psychology and neuroscience that seem to diminish the cognitive competence of the individual. (We will see how more humanistic researchers and writers reinforce these impressions in their own way in the next chapter.)

If we read that researchers have found evidence—or, in the language of the popular media, have "proven"—that we can't make good decisions, then it's reasonable for us to conclude that maybe we should cede decisions to someone else. If we read that researchers say our happiness is measurable and that they've derived observations from these measurements, then it's reasonable to conclude that maybe my happiness is not the unique personal experience I thought it was. If Netflix seems to be able to predict which movie we're going to watch next, it's reasonable to conclude that their algorithms know our preferences and desires as well as we do (or maybe even better). We only think this way, though, because we do not realize or appreciate how rich and complex our interests and choices are—and as we saw so far in this book, neither do the researchers whose work reinforces that misconception.

A greater awareness of the rich complexity of our interests, judgment, and choices by all parties involved could lead to better research, more nuanced reporting on that research, and policies more respectful of individual interests and choices. The science underlying all of these societal developments holds tremendous promise for improving the lives of individuals and the prosperity of society (as defined by the individuals who comprise it), but as with all scientific and technological developments, ethics is necessary to make sure they are reported, interpreted, and put into practice in a way that respects individuals.

More importantly, this greater awareness could lead to a greater appreciation of ourselves as valuable and unique persons and give us a better foundation from which to understand, interpret, and when necessary push back again these new methods of policy and commerce. Cass Sunstein was correct when he said that sometimes, it is better to choose not to choose, but so was Rush when they sang that when we choose not to decide, we still have made a choice. We can certainly cede our choices to others, but that higher level, "meta" choice should be a conscious and deliberate one. Will Davies points out that the new behavioral science may be welcomed by some people because it seems to relieve them of the burden of making choices themselves.[54] After all, if someone else can make our decisions for us, or if we believe our choices are determined by environmental factors in general and out of our control, that may be quite a load off! And it's true that, as philosopher Christine Korsgaard wrote, "human beings are *condemned* to choice and action."[55] We cannot avoid choice, even if we choose not to choose. But if we too easily give up our responsibility to make choices for ourselves, we give up an essential component of ourselves as individuals —our ability to craft who we are with the choices we make.

None of this is to say that any of us should presume to be an island. I am not promoting individualism in the sense that each of us should go into the world alone to make of ourselves what we can. Absolutely not: I firmly believe that in most circumstances, we can achieve much more together than we can separately. What I am promoting is *individuality*, the idea that each of us is a unique person with a responsibility to be authentic to who we want to be, even when—and especially when—we work together on common goals. This balance of individuality and sociality will be the focus of the next chapter, as we turn our attention away from science and technology to confront some thinkers on the humanistic side of the fence who question the concept of individuality and the *moral* competence of individuals. Luckily, we will have the support of some old philosopher friends to craft our defense of a more nuanced and elaborate vision of the individual, including one we just Kant do without.

Notes

1. See "Computers in Spaceflight: The NASA Experience," at https://history.nasa.gov/computers/Part1.html, and Cliff Saran, "Apollo 11: The computers that put man on the moon," ComputerWeekly.com, July 2009, at http://www.computerweekly.com/feature/Apollo-11-The-computers-that-put-man-on-the-moon.
2. See Wolf's TED talk here: http://www.ted.com/talks/gary_wolf_the_quantified_self. On the quantified self, see also April Dembosky, "Invasion of the Body Hackers," *Financial Times*, June 10, 2011, at https://www.ft.com/content/3ccb11a0-923b-11e0-9e00-00144feab49a, and Emily Singer, "The Measured Life," *MIT Technology Review*, June 21, 2011, at https://www.technologyreview.com/s/424390/the-measured-life/.
3. For example, see Sandra Aamodt, "Why You Can't Lose Weight on a Diet," *The New York Times*, May 6, 2016, at https://www.nytimes.com/2016/05/08/opinion/sunday/why-you-cant-lose-weight-on-a-diet.html.
4. David Beer, *Metric Power* (London: Palgrave Macmillan, 2016), p. 3.
5. Ibid., pp. 6–7; see also pp. 60–69 on biometrics in general.
6. Luigi Doria, *Calculating the Human: Universal Calculability in the Age of Quality Assurance* (London: Palgrave Macmillan, 2013), p. 1: "Calculation tends to encompass 'objects'… which historically have been at its periphery. … [And] precisely when we are faced with the calculation of the incalculable human, the awkward question of the unconditional character of calculation is projected as a disturbing shadows."
7. On this, see my book *The Illusion of Well-Being: Economic Policymaking Based on Respect and Responsiveness* (New York: Palgrave Macmillan, 2014).

8. While this quote is often attributed to Albert Einstein—aren't they all?—it is more likely due to William Bruce Cameron: "Not everything that can be counted counts, and not everything that counts can be counted" (*Informal Sociology: A Casual Introduction to Sociological Thinking*, New York: Random House, 1963, p. 13). See the Quote Investigator at http://quoteinvestigator.com/2010/05/26/everything-counts-einstein.
9. Even worse, they can exacerbate other problems, such as eating disorders; see Katherine Schreiber, "Do Fitness Trackers Promote Eating Disorders?", *Psychology Today*, February 15, 2017, at https://www.psychologytoday.com/blog/the-truth-about-exercise-addiction/201702/do-fitness-trackers-promote-eating-disorders.
10. Adam Smith, *An Inquiry into the Nature and Causes of the Wealth of Nations* (1776), available from the Library of Economics and Liberty at http://www.econlib.org/library/Smith/smWN.html. For an insightful look into Smith's most famous concept, see Jonathan B. Wight, "The Treatment of Smith's Invisible Hand," *Journal of Economic Education* 38 (2007): 341–358.
11. Cass R. Sunstein, *Choosing Not to Choose* (Oxford: Oxford University Press, 2015).
12. Dirk Helbing, Bruno S. Frey, Gerd Gigerenzer, Ernst Hafen, Michael Hagner, Yvonne Hofstetter, Jeroen van den Hoven, Roberto V. Zicari, and Andrej Zwitter, "Will Democracy Survive Big Data and Artificial Intelligence," *Scientific American*, February 25, 2017, at https://www.scientificamerican.com/article/will-democracy-survive-big-data-and-artificial-intelligence/. In the worst case scenario, they argue, computers may control us more directly and thoroughly. Drawing an analogy to nudge politics (discussed in the last chapter), they write that: "Some software platforms are moving towards 'persuasive computing.' In the future, using sophisticated manipulation technologies, these platforms will be able to steer us through entire courses of action, be it for the execution of complex work processes or to generate free content for Internet platforms, from which corporations earn billions. *The trend goes from programming computers to programming people.*"
13. David Beer, "Algorithms: the villains and heroes of the 'post-truth' era," *openDemocracy*, January 3, 2017, at https://www.opendemocracy.net/digitaliberties/david-beer/algorithms-villains-and-heroes-of-post-truth-era ; in general, see Frank Pasquale, *The Black Box Society: The Secret Algorithms That Control Money and Information* (Cambridge, MA: Harvard University Press, 2015), chapter 3.
14. Before that annoying person in the back of the room raises his hand, yes, of course I know that true objectivity in journalism (or anything) is impossible

because journalists can never escape their own point of view or unconscious biases. Objectivity is an impossible ideal, but it is still one worth striving for.

15. For example, see Adam Pasick, "Facebook says it can sway elections after all—for a price," *Quartz*, March 1, 2017, at https://qz.com/922436/facebook-says-it-can-sway-elections-after-all-for-a-price/; David Shultz, "Could Google influence the presidential election?", *Science*, October 25, 2016, at http://www.sciencemag.org/news/2016/10/could-google-influence-presidential-election.

16. For example, see Bill Bishop, *The Big Sort: Why the Clustering of Like-Minded America Is Tearing Us Apart* (New York: Houghton Mifflin Harcourt, 2008); Cass R. Sunstein, *#Republic: Divided Democracy in an Age of Social Media* (Princeton, NJ: Princeton University Press, 2017).

17. George Dyson, *Turing's Cathedral: The Origins of the Digital Universe* (New York: Pantheon, 2012), p. 308.

18. Nate Silver, *The Signal and the Noise: Why So Many Predictions Fail—But Some Don't* (New York: Penguin, 2012), p. 9.

19. In fact, Vox has a page at its site explaining how it aggregates the news it presents and explains: http://www.vox.com/2015/4/13/8405999/how-vox-aggregates.

20. Cathy O'Neil, *Weapons of Math Destruction: How Big Data Increases Inequality and Threatens Democracy* (New York: Crown, 2016), p. 3.

21. Theodore M. Porter, *Trust in Numbers: The Pursuit of Objectivity in Science and Public Life* (Princeton, NJ: Princeton University Press, 1995), p. ix; for more on objectivity, see chapter 1.

22. Beer, *Metric Power*, pp. 137–138.

23. Will Davies, *The Limits of Neoliberalism* (London: Sage, 2014), p. 16.

24. See Kenneth S. Rogoff, *The Curse of Cash* (Princeton, NJ: Princeton University Press, 2016), especially Part I, "The Dark Side of Paper Currency: Tax and Regulatory Evasion, Crime, and Security Issues."

25. Never mind the fact that data from Fitbits and other personal devices (such as digital personal assistants like Alexa and Siri) have already been used in court; for example, see Kate Crawford, "When Fitbit Is the Expert Witness," *The Atlantic*, November 19, 2014, at https://www.theatlantic.com/technology/archive/2014/11/when-fitbit-is-the-expert-witness/382936/, and Gerald Sauer, "A Murder Case Tests Alexa's Devotion to Your Privacy," *Wired*, February 28, 2017, at https://www.wired.com/2017/02/murder-case-tests-alexas-devotion-privacy/.

26. Pasquale, *Black Box Society*.

27. Ibid., p. 10.

28. Beer, *Metric Power*, p. 136. There is some sign of backlash, although not necessarily for the right reasons; see Will Davies, "How Statistics Lost Their Power—And Why We Should Fear What Comes Next," *The Guardian*,

January 19, 2017, at https://www.theguardian.com/politics/2017/jan/19/crisis-of-statistics-big-data-democracy.

29. Hannah Arendt, *Crises of the Republic* (New York: Harcourt Brace and Company, 1972), p. 37. For a modern look at algorithms in wartime decision-making, see the "War-Algorithm Accountability" report produced by the Harvard Law School Program on International Law and Armed Conflict (PILAC), at https://pilac.law.harvard.edu/waa.

30. Beer, *Metric Power*, p. 181. See the story of the teacher rating system in Washington D.C., recounted by O'Neil in chapter 1 of *Weapons of Mass Destruction*: when a teacher was wrongly dismissed because of the failure of the rating algorithm to account for all the facts of her case, she was nonetheless told the process was "fair," and she had "only" her story to counter her accusers' numbers. As O'Neil writes, victims of algorithms "are held to a far higher standard of evidence than the algorithms themselves" (p. 10).

31. Sally Eagle Merry, *The Seductions of Quantification: Measuring Human Rights, Gender Violence, and Sex Trafficking* (Chicago: University of Chicago Press, 2016), p. 5.

32. O'Neil, *Weapons of Math Destruction*, chapter 5. See also Pasquale, *Black Box Society*, pp. 38–42; David Black, "Big Data on the Beat," *City Journal*, Winter 2016, at https://www.city-journal.org/html/big-data-beat-14125.html; and Robert Muggah, "What happens when we can predict crimes before they happen?", *World Economic Forum*, February 2, 2017, at https://www.weforum.org/agenda/2017/02/what-happens-when-we-can-predict-crimes-before-they-happen/.

33. Pasquale, *Black Box Society*, p. 42.

34. For example, see O'Neil, *Weapons of Math Destruction*, pp. 100–104. See also Pasquale, *Black Box Society*, p. 21, which tells of a woman who was visited by members of a terrorism task force after she searched online for the term "pressure cooker" and her husband searched for "backpacks"; and Ava Kofman, "Taser Will Use Police Body Camera Videos 'To Anticipate Criminal Activity,'" *The Intercept*, April 30, 2017, at https://theintercept.com/2017/04/30/taser-will-use-police-body-camera-videos-to-anticipate-criminal-activity/. (Taser International is the world's largest seller of police body cameras.)

35. O'Neil, *Weapons of Math Destruction*, pp. 23–27; see also the Electronic Privacy Information Center's undated report on "Algorithms in the Criminal Justice System" at https://epic.org/algorithmic-transparency/crim-justice/.

36. See also Adam Liptak, "Sent to Prison by a Software Program's Secret Algorithms," *The New York Times*, May 1, 2017, at https://www.

nytimes.com/2017/05/01/us/politics/sent-to-prison-by-a-software-programs-secret-algorithms.html.
37. For more on this, see *The Illusion of Well-Being*, chapter 1; for other critiques, see Will Davies, *The Happiness Industry: How the Government and Big Business Sold Us Well-Being* (London: Verso, 2015).
38. Nicholas Eberstadt, *The Tyranny of Numbers: Mismeasurement and Misrule* (Washington, DC: The AEI Press, 1995), p. 2; Pitirim Sorokin, *Fads and Foibles in Modern Sociology and Related Sciences* (Chicago: Henry Regnery Company, 1956). For examples of the problems with quantitative governance, see the bulk of Eberstadt's book; Merry, *Seductions of Quantification*; O'Neil, *Weapons of Math Destruction*; and Richard Rottenberg, Sally E. Merry, Sung-Joon Park, and Johanna Mugler (eds.), *The World of Indicators: The Making of Governmental Knowledge through Quantification* (Cambridge: Cambridge University Press, 2015).
39. Eberstadt, *Tyranny of Numbers*, p. 26.
40. Merry, *Seductions of Quantification*, pp. 3–4. (I wish I'd thought of that title!) On pp. 19–22, Merry explores the "myth of objectivity," based on *false specificity* (that numbers seem to lend precision to rough measurements) and the *masking of political origin* ("indicators are subtly and even unconsciously shaped by the assumptions, motivations, and concerns of those who carry them out").
41. Ibid., pp. 221–222.
42. Porter, *Trust in Numbers*, p. 85.
43. O'Neil, *Weapons of Math Destruction*, p. 204 (emphasis added).
44. My brief discussion here does not cover the shortcomings of GDP as a measure of well-being, such as its failure to account for unpaid work, inequality, or lack of freedoms, all of which are covered in most introductory economics texts and nicely surveyed in Joseph E. Stiglitz, Amartya Sen, and Jean-Paul Fitoussi, *Mismeasuring Our Lives: Why GDP Doesn't Add Up* (New York: New Press, 2010) and Dirk Philipsen, *The Little Big Number: How GDP Came to Rule the World and What to Do about It* (Princeton, NJ: Princeton University Press, 2015). For fascinating reads on the history and thinking behind GDP, see Diane Coyle, *GDP: A Brief but Affectionate History* (Princeton, NJ: Princeton University Press, 2014); Philipp Lepenies, *The Power of a Single Number: A Political History of GDP* (New York: Columbia University Press, 2016); and Ehsan Mahmood, *The Great Invention: The Story of GDP and the Making (and Unmaking) of the Modern World* (New York: Pegasus, 2016).
45. Immanuel Kant, *Grounding for the Metaphysics of Morals*, translated by James W. Ellington (Indianapolis, IN: Hackett Publishing Company, 1785/1993), p. 434; the persons/things distinction itself appears on

p. 428. See also Roger J. Sullivan, *Immanuel Kant's Moral Theory* (Cambridge: Cambridge University Press, 1989), pp. 195–198.
46. Beer, *Metric Power*, p. 57.
47. Merry, *Seduction of Quantification*, p. 1. Even the census—literally a counting of heads—is inherently political; see Porter, *Trust in Numbers*, pp. 34–37, and Sarah Igo, *The Averaged American: Surveys, Citizens, and the Making of a Mass Public* (Cambridge, MA: Harvard University, 2007), pp. 296–299.
48. Porter, *Trust in Numbers*, p. 77. Others who have written on the coercive power of statistics, many of them inspired by Michael Foucault's work on statistics in governance, include Ian Hacking, *Taming of Chance* (Cambridge: Cambridge University Press, 1990); Nikolas Rose, *Governing the Soul* (London: Routledge, 1990); Beer, *Metric Power*; and Davies, *The Happiness Industry* and *The Limits of Neoliberalism*.
49. Stuart Elden, *Speaking Against Number: Heidegger, Language and the Politics of Calculation* (Edinburgh: Edinburgh University Press, 2006), p. 180.
50. William Irwin, *The Free Market Existentialist: Capitalism without Consumerism* (Malden, MA: Wiley Blackwell, 2015), p. 63. I thought I had come up with this nice turn of phrase myself, but upon re-reading Irwin's book after drafting this one, I had to admit I probably got it from him. (Happy now, Bill?)
51. Jeremy Bentham, *The Principles of Morals and Legislation* (Buffalo, NY: Prometheus Books, 1781/1988); John Stuart Mill, *Utilitarianism* (Oxford: Oxford University Press, 1863/1998). Both are available online at https://www.utilitarianism.com.
52. John Rawls, *A Theory of Justice* (Cambridge, MA: Harvard University Press, 1971), p. 27.
53. The trolley problem, originally proposed by Philippa Foot and developed by Judith Jarvis Thomson, has received a significant amount of attention in recent years. See, for example, Thomas Cathcart, *The Trolley Problem—or —Would You Throw the Fat Guy Off the Bridge?* (New York: Workman, 2013); David Edmonds, *Would You Kill the Fat Man?* (Princeton, NJ: Princeton University Press, 2014); and F.M. Kamm, *The Trolley Problem Mysteries* (Oxford: Oxford University Press, 2016). Predating this recent work is your own correspondent's chapter "Why Doesn't Batman Kill the Joker?" in Mark D. White and Robert Arp (eds.), *Batman and Philosophy: The Dark Knight of the Soul* (Hoboken, NJ: Wiley Blackwell, 2008), pp. 5–16.
54. Davies, *Happiness Industry*, p. 90.
55. Christine Korsgaard, *Self-Constitution: Agency, Identity, and Integrity* (Oxford: Oxford University Press, 2009), p. 1.

CHAPTER 4

Individual in Essence, Social in Orientation

The last two chapters of this book described advancements in science and technology that, while valuable in and of themselves, have the effect of diminishing the respect we have for the individual. They do so in two ways: by too broadly questioning our cognitive competency, based on an overly simplistic understanding of decision-making processes, and reducing human lives to their most quantifiable aspects, leading both us and other parties to focus on those parts of life that can be put into the form of numbers and ignoring the rich complexity of the rest.

The cumulative effect of these developments is to cast doubt on our ability to make sound decisions in our interests, doubt on our own behalf as well as on the part of other institutions such as business and government. By reducing human behavior to simple goals, drives, and influences, all based on limited observation interpreted through the lens of theoretical preconceptions, these developments cast human decision-making in a pessimistic light that influences the actions of business, government, and, most importantly, ourselves, in a vicious circle in which doubt validates itself and justifies the interference with our choices by others who do not know our true interests.

It is not only science working against respect for the individual, but a more humanistic outlook as well. Recently, scholars and commentators writing from the perspective of philosophy, political science, and sociology, as well as the more humanistic sides of psychology and neuroscience, also serve to diminish the value and standing of the individual. Reinforcing the impressions left by the scientific and technological trends described in the last two chapters, these writers examine the place of individual in society as a whole. But just as the scientists painted individuals as irrational in their choices regarding themselves, the humanistic writers describe individuals as being similarly flawed in the ethical or social dimension. They describe the individual as inherently antisocial and selfish, questioning the moral competence of individuals in the same way that scientists question their cognitive competence. Taken together, these scholars and writers feel that individuals are doomed to make poor choices not only on their own behalf, but on behalf of society as a whole.

The picture of the individual painted by writers from a more humanistic view is even more simplistic than that presumed by scientists. As I will explain in this chapter, this image of the individual as an isolated, antisocial, and purely self-interested hermit is a caricature, pushing the individual to one extreme in order to argue for a better world at the other, a world in which individuals are wholly subsumed by the society they make up (and the government that oversees it). This is basically the economic model of choice taken at its most simplistic, and we'll see that the criticisms that have been leveled at economics' picture of the individual apply here as well.

In place of this straw man, I propose a more elaborate and subtle understanding of the individual and his or her place within society, one that respects individuals' autonomy as well as their responsibility toward their fellow human beings: *individual in essence, social in orientation*. By this, I mean that individuals make their own choices, exercising their autonomy, in ways that respect and support the autonomy and interests of others. There is no contradiction between autonomy and altruism; autonomy does not imply selfishness, and altruism does not rely on coordination or incentives provided by the state. Individuals can act socially and still remain individuals, making choices in an environment of mutual respect and concern—and this understanding is essential to correct mistaken caricatures as well as reverse the decline in respect for the individual.

INDIVIDUALS ARE SOCIAL—BUT ARE WE SOCIAL ENOUGH?

It is commonplace these days to hear that we are inherently social beings. This is nothing new; in times of antiquity, Aristotle wrote that "man is by nature a political animal" and attributed our power of speech, seen as unique among the animals (at least in advanced form), as endowed by nature so we could communicate, cooperate, and judge right from wrong.[1] Immanuel Kant spoke of human beings' *"unsocial sociability,"* i.e., their tendency to enter into society, combined, however, with a thoroughgoing resistance that constantly threatens to sunder this society."[2] Our drive to be with others and to be accepted as part of society conflicts with our own wants and desires and, more essentially, our need to be ourselves at the same time. And of course, describing the existentialist dilemma of defining one's own essence in the face of others doing the same—another inescapable aspect of interpersonal conflict—existentialist philosopher Jean-Paul Sartre famously wrote that "hell is other people."[3]

More recently, science has reinforced the social nature of the individual. Evolutionary biologists, psychologists, and neuroscientists agree that we evolved together, surviving best in (small) groups and thereby developing natural propensities for altruism and reciprocity.[4] However, this social coexistence isn't always smooth or easy, as the human race's experiences with violence, war, and slavery show all too tragically. Furthermore, because we evolved in small communities, we developed a deep mistrust of "the other," which today reveals itself in inherent racism, if not explicit hostility and conflict.[5] Similar to the morally benign cognitive biases we surveyed earlier, these are evolved antisocial dispositions that we need to acknowledge and resist, especially if we hope to treat each other with respect and empathy.[6]

In general, as philosophy, science, and our history as a species all demonstrate, human beings have always found it difficult to reconcile our sociality with our individuality. This plays out on a very personal level, as small numbers of us bond in family, friendships, and romantic ties, and on a broader societal level, in which large numbers of us interact in the context of community, church, and politics. However much (or little) we want to be with other people, we do so as individuals, always separate even when we want—or need—to be together. In the words of the Buddhist writer and author Stephen Bachelor, we are always "alone with others."[7]

According to the prevailing opinion, the uncomfortable struggle behind the individual and society is being won by the former, as a "radical individualism" threatens the social fabric. It is common to read narratives, anecdotes, and statistics bemoaning how, on average, people spend more time alone and less time with others; have more "Facebook friends" but fewer close friends in real life, leading, in the worst cases, to chronic and life-threatening loneliness; and are less active in social institutions such as community groups and church activities.[8] These trends are blamed for various social ills, such as a decrease in personal happiness or well-being, a decline in trust in government, and even the growth of neofascist movements and terrorism.[9] The pendulum has swung too far, critics say, turning from a fidelity to God, community, and country, to a self-focused individualism that threatens the close bonds that we need as a species to survive and prosper.

You'll hardly be surprised to hear that when I would tell friends and colleagues about this book I was writing, they would be amused (at best) that I was going to argue *in favor of* the importance of the individual. "Haven't we put the individual first for long enough?" they would ask. "Isn't the focus on the individual the real problem today?" These are reasonable questions, and the fact that they're so common—and that the answer to both, in my opinion, is so clearly "no"—highlights the need for a more elaborate and nuanced understanding of individuals and their role in society.

The problems listed above are real and serious, and the social (and not so social) trends identified by scholars and commentators are worrisome. But I dispute that a strong sense of the individual is to blame; rather, a distorted picture of the individual often lurks beneath the scenes of such critiques, one that denies each individual's inherent ability to be social and, at the time, autonomous.

This signals what is perhaps the most significant barrier to appreciating the nature and value of the individual: the false dichotomy between the individual and society that is so prevalent in our thinking today. It is present in my friends' and colleagues' questions above and is more forcibly argued in much of the commentary and scholarship coming from the humanities on the issue. When we cast the individual against society as if in a winner-takes-all cage match, naturally the better choice would seem to be society. But it is not one or the other; they are both crucial and need to be combined in a way that acknowledges the unique ways in which each is important. Presenting a false dichotomy between them helps no one and makes it more difficult to appreciate how they work together.

David Brooks and the False Dichotomy

One of the most well-known critics of the modern individual outside of the academy is the bestselling author, popular speaker, and columnist for *The New York Times*, David Brooks. In many of his columns as well as his books—especially *The Social Animal*—Brooks has challenged what he sees as excessive individualism in modern American society.[10] Like the other scholars and commentators mentioned above, he argues that we focus too much on ourselves and not enough on others, that we've become unmoored from civic life and community institutions (both religious and secular), and that we've grown more miserable because this self-imposed isolation has led us to a crisis of meaning in which we find it more difficult to connect with something larger than ourselves. Calling back to the greater connectedness of the mid-twentieth century, Brooks calls for a rejection of individualistic, self-centered, and shallow pursuits and a renewed devotion to community, politics, and meaningful, socially oriented activities, all encouraged and promoted by government (when necessary).

Much of this is unobjectionable and even agreeable, and Brooks bases his opinions on a wealth of research from psychology, economics, sociology, and other fields (as the copious references in *The Social Animal* well attest). Yes, individuals are generally happier and feel more fulfilled the more they engage in activities that benefit others, provided that they do so sincerely or not strategically. Such activities are often essential to the sense of meaning and purpose that leads to the deeper sense of happiness that the ancient philosophers called *eudaimonia*. In terms of present-oriented pleasures—which are important as well—most people are generally happier the more time they spend with others, although there are differences in terms of how individuals like to interact with others (small versus large groups, short versus long time periods, and so on). Finally, in these times of bitter divisiveness, I would certainly like to see a greater sense of community, if only to expose people of different mind-sets to each other and generate civil dialogue to promote better understanding and tolerance (if not agreement).

My main point of disagreement with Mr. Brooks may be described as more rhetorical, in terms of how he characterizes the individual in contrast to society. As he describes the modern individual, his picture resembles the simplest version of *homo economicus*, the hypothetical person of traditional economic models whom we met in an earlier chapter. This person—let's call him Hank—considers himself self-made, giving no credit or acknowledgement to those who helped him or came before, and only thinks of himself, never of others. Hank is concerned only with his freedom, his ability to choose from as many options as he can have, and wants as few restrictions as possible on them. According to Brooks, these ideas were instilled in Hank from an early age, by a society (parents, teachers, political leaders) who taught him that self-fulfillment and expression were the most important goals: "Follow your passion, chart your own course, march to the beat of your own drummer, follow your dreams and find yourself. This is the litany of expressive individualism, which is still the dominant note in American culture."[11] Hank is the mythical "self-made man" who depends on no one else, needs no one else, and thinks of no one else.[12]

This vision of the individual as isolated and independent is often referred to as "atomistic," although this is unfair to atoms, which form bonds with each other all the time! The idea behind the term is that the atomistic individual floats through the world, not interacting with other individuals nor being affected by them except insofar as they provide information that can be used to his advantage. The term is also used in critical discussions of *homo economicus* by other economists and social scientists. In his most basic form, *homo economicus*—or Hank—makes choices to maximally satisfy his preferences (which are granted to him rather than influenced by others) within his available resources (similarly granted to him or acquired through previous choices). His preferences are normally based on his own self-interest, ranking options according to which ones will give him more satisfaction or utility. As we saw earlier, these preferences can include altruistic concerns, but these are not usually included in the standard picture of *homo economicus*, nor in Brooks' conception of the modern individual.

This model will be familiar to students of microeconomics, where it is presented as a problem to be solved either graphically, with indifference curves and a budget line, or mathematically, with the logic of marginal analysis. Either way, it is a mechanistic process, one in which preferences are assessed against resources and the optimal solution is "found"—no *real* choice involved here—and one that is thoroughly isolated in that it focuses solely on Hank. He does need to get some information from his environment, most importantly the costs of the various options he has to choose from, as well as the qualities of those options (which form the basis of the satisfaction he gets from them). But this does not make other persons necessary to the process: The typical example of the truly independent economic agent, Robinson Crusoe, makes choices alone on a desert island using marginal analysis. In typical economic models, other people are needed only for trade, which is important in that it enables individuals to increase their satisfaction or utility through taking advantage of the unique preferences and endowments of each person, but not for social purposes in and of themselves.

While this model has been standard in economics for the last century, there are critics from within the field who take exception with the asocial nature of *homo economicus*. Social economists, for example, emphasize that individuals do not make decisions in isolation from other people. In their view, economics is an integral and inseparable part of society, and social considerations are inherent in all choices individuals make.[13] They often draw from the work of their close cousins, economic sociologists, who argue that individuals are "socially embedded," a concept that criticizes (among other things) the atomistic individual and the idea that his preferences are wholly his own and not a product of social influences.[14] Social economists use their framework to argue for the importance of recognizing and incorporating social values and ethics in economic theory, policy, and practice, and this serves as an important counterpoint to the simplistic asocial nature of *homo economicus*. (In other words, they would agree with Brooks that Hank should make some friends.)

However valid Brooks' criticisms of the modern individual are, he succumbs to a false dichotomy regarding how the individual in general relates to society. For example, in *The Social Animal*, he criticizes the visions of individualism promoted by both the political right and left:

> They both had individualistic worldviews, tending to assume that society was a contract between autonomous individuals. Both promoted policies designed to expand individual choice. Neither paid much attention to social and communal bonds, to local associations, or invisible norms. ... For a generation, no matter who was in power, the prevailing winds had been blowing in the direction of autonomy, individualism, and personal freedom, not in the direction of society, social obligations, and communal bonds.[15]

Earlier in his book, one of Brooks' main characters, Harold, has a similar epiphany that, despite his inculcation in this culture of "expressive individualism, self-fulfillment, and personal liberation," he realized—after 40 years!—that he needed "more community, connection, and interpenetration" to be happy. "He couldn't bring out his best self alone. He could only do it in conjunction with other people."[16]

These passages are reminiscent of Brooks' columns in *The New York Times* over the years regarding how the individual relates to society, casting "autonomy, individualism, and personal freedom" against "society, social obligations, and communal bonds." Even if his observations about modern individuals as we see them today are accurate, these facts have more to do with their specific behavior, motivations, and goals than with their essential faculties of autonomous choice, which should not be contrasted with more social aspects of life but can and often does incorporate them. Autonomy and individuality do not deny "conjunction with other people," as Harold thought—they can easily welcome and embrace it.

Just because individuals make choices autonomously does not mean they necessarily make them selfishly or shortsightedly. As we've seen, people make smart decisions and they make stupid decisions; they make callously selfish decisions and they make altruistic decisions involving tremendous sacrifice. But these can all be autonomous decisions, which does not fit Brooks' conception of the individual in either empirical or abstract terms.

For example, in his column "It's Not About You," Brooks draws on college graduation speeches, noting that they often promote a self-centered worldview. He cites the surgeon and writer Atul Gawande as sending a different message to graduates, one of cooperation and teamwork as opposed to rugged individualism:

> Finally, graduates are told to be independent-minded and to express their inner spirit. But, of course, doing your job well often means suppressing yourself. As Atul Gawande mentioned during his countercultural address last week at Harvard Medical School, being a good doctor often means being part of a team, following the rules of an institution, going down a regimented checklist.[17]

Once again, this is a false dichotomy. In fact, individuals *can* make autonomous choices to join a team and follow rules. These are valid paths to follow in one's own self-determination or, in philosopher Christine Korsgaard's terms, *self-constitution*; later in this chapter, we will see how she wrote of the importance of the roles we accept and how we integrate those various roles into a self that we can endorse.[18]

In the same spirit, autonomy can also involve commitment, whether to a career, a cause, or another person. In a column about same-sex marriage, published before the 2015 *Obergefell* decision by the Supreme Court that recognized it as law, Brooks lauded the movement in support of marriage equalization as a movement *away* from freedom and autonomy:

> …last week saw a setback for the forces of maximum freedom. A representative of millions of gays and lesbians went to the Supreme Court and asked the court to help put limits on their own freedom of choice. They asked for marriage.

4 INDIVIDUAL IN ESSENCE, SOCIAL IN ORIENTATION

> Marriage is one of those institutions—along with religion and military service—that restricts freedom. Marriage is about making a commitment that binds you for decades to come. It narrows your options on how you will spend your time, money and attention.
>
> Whether they understood it or not, the gays and lesbians represented at the court committed themselves to a certain agenda. They committed themselves to an institution that involves surrendering autonomy.[19]

Rather than seeing self-constraint as a rejection of autonomy, however, we can see it as the ultimate expression of it. People make conscious, deliberate, reflective—and autonomous—decisions to limit their future options all the time, whether by agreeing to a job, signing up for military service, or saying "I do" to another person. Any of these choices involve sacrificing some freedoms, and they are all made, in ideal circumstances, in the full spirit of autonomy. Indeed, in Immanuel Kant's conception, autonomy is *all about* holding yourself to the constraints implied by the moral law, which can include constraints we make on ourselves through promises or commitments.

All these examples from Brooks' work reinforce a false dichotomy that sets the individual against the society in which he or she lives and thrives. It mischaracterizes autonomy and freedom by casting it in the most reductive and limited arena, that of narrowly focused pursuit of self-interest, or what usually passes for "individualism." To the contrary, autonomy and freedom allow individuals to pursue their interests to the fullest extent possible, whatever those interests may be—including committing oneself to causes much bigger than yourself, or to the person standing beside you when you make wedding vows. Brooks is correct to point out that modern individuals need more sociality in their lives, but he is wrong to think this means giving up individuality, autonomy, or freedom. If anything, sociality, if it is going to be meaningful and beneficial, *needs* to be selected autonomously and freely—as anyone who was forced to play with their little cousin "whether you like it or not" knows all too well.

INDIVIDUAL IN ESSENCE...

There's a better way to think about the individual, one that combines individuality and sociality in a way that recognizes the unique importance of each. After much consultation with marketing experts and dozens of focus groups—and then ignoring their advice—I arrived at this phrase:

individual in essence, social in orientation. In short, this captures my view that a person is both individual and social but in different ways. At our core, we are individuals, making decisions in our complex and multifaceted interests; at the same time, those interests may and should include respect and concern for other people. In short, we make our own decisions as autonomous individuals, but this does not mean those decisions must be selfish in nature; they are and should be socially minded. In what follows, I hope to dispel the notion that a strong sense of the individual denies that he or she can be social at the same time.

What do I mean by "individual in essence"? There are several dimensions to this, but the most basic one is that we are, physically and mentally, separate beings. As much as we might join together in groups and cooperate on shared projects, each of us is an individual, separate from each other. You do not have to accept a purely physical theory of the mind to appreciate that our mental activity takes place in our brains, which are securely housed in our skulls.[20] When I decided to write this book or you decided to read it, that was a choice made by me or you—perhaps influenced by others, as we will see later, but the decision itself was ultimately mine or yours.

I don't want to belabor this point, which seems obvious, but is nonetheless underappreciated. Consider when we say things such as having a "meeting of the minds" or "putting our heads together" to solve a problem. Those are nice metaphors, but they are exactly that: ways to think of cooperation that will overcome the brute fact that our brains are separate entities. Someday, we may develop technology to mimic the Vulcan mind meld (from *Star Trek*) or the hive mind of the Borg (also from *Star Trek*), but even those remote possibilities only serve to highlight the fact that there is a distance between our minds that has to be overcome by some form of communication.[21]

On top of the physical fact of the separateness of our brains is a deeper moral aspect of our individuality. For this, we will once again draw on Immanuel Kant, whose moral philosophy grounds my conception of the individual (as well as many other concepts in this book).[22] One of the most important foundational concepts in Kant's ethics is *autonomy*, which grounds his assertion that persons, unlike things, have dignity and therefore command respect (which leads to the categorical imperative and the duties derived from it). While autonomy has many different meanings today, ranging from the personal to the political, Kant has one specific meaning in mind: To him, autonomy describes our capacity as rational beings to make moral decisions independently of both internal desires and external pressures.

Both aspects of Kantian autonomy are essential to its meaning. First, autonomy means not being slaves to our own desires; we must be able to make ethical choices regardless of our personal preferences. In simple terms, we must be able to "do the right thing" even when we don't want to—or *especially* when we don't want to. (After all, it's easy to do the right thing when doing so would also work out well for us.) To be truly autonomous, we must be able to put our moral code above our own desires, accepting that it's more important to do the right thing than the thing we want to do. This is likely a familiar conflict for most of us, being caught between what we want to do and what we feel we should do, whether for other people or for our own future selves in terms of long-term health or financial well-being. While we usually think of autonomy in relation to other people, this internal aspect of autonomy shows that our true moral selves should be free from our desires—and anyone who has struggled to resist that second piece of cake, give that extra dollar in change back to the cashier, or ignore that cute person across the room at our engagement party, recognizes the importance of this side of autonomy.

If we go deeper into this, we see that not only does autonomy demand that we act contrary to our desires when ethics demands it, but it may also call into question our desires themselves, many of which come from external sources, whether or not we realize it and whether or not we've endorsed them as our own. As we saw earlier, many scholars from various fields study the processes by which individuals' preferences are formed; regardless of the details of the mechanisms by which this happens, it remains that many of our tastes and desires are influenced by external factors.[23] The most obvious of these is advertising, the purpose of which is to develop in consumers a preference for a product in order to boost sales. But our desires are shaped also by many less overt aspects of our environment, especially our social worlds, including the people we associate with, the experiences we have, and the culture we're brought up and live in. This is not to say these influences are bad—far from it! I'll always be grateful to the people, places, and experiences that exposed me to the music, films, books, and foods I love. And even after our basic tastes are formed—say, for heavy metal, romcoms, historical fiction, and Thai food—they are further refined not only by our own explorations but by other people and the specific examples of these tastes that they expose us to.

As sociologists know well, our social world is an important and integral part of how to discover what we like and what preference we develop.[24] At the same time, however, we must reflect upon and endorse these preferences rather than simply accepting them unconditionally. No one is going to adopt a taste for mushrooms simply because someone tells them to (especially considering that they're revolting).[25] But some may be pressured into liking, or pretending to like, a style of music or genre of film because it's popular or cool, and sometimes, we may simply adopt the tastes and preferences of our family or friends without thinking about it: "It's just what we do." While doing this may ease some social anxiety or help us make new friends, it's not authentic to who we are or who we want to be, unless we reflectively consider those preferences and consciously integrate them into our concept of our selves. It may be harmless if we only do it occasionally to ease into a new social group, but if we do it too much, there's a danger of subordinating our tastes and preferences to those of others, similar to doing anything else someone tells us to do just because they tell us to do it.

This is only one way that a person can be an individual while at the time inherently social. The individual in this conception does not ignore the world around her, like the isolated, self-reliant, "radical individual" does. Instead, she embraces it and endorses it when it corresponds to who she is or wants to be as a person. She adopts tastes when they appeal to her, not just when they are popular; she follows recommendations or commands when she feels they are in keeping with her moral code; and she sets aside her own desires and preferences when she realizes that doing the right thing is more important. She decides what kind of person she's going to be and creates that person—not out of whole cloth and not without influence from the outside world, but considering these influences while acting as final arbiter on which influences she's going to incorporate and which she's going to reject. As philosopher John Stuart Mill wrote, "it is the privilege and proper condition of a human being, arrived at the maturity of his faculties, to use and interpret experience in his own way. It is for him to find out what part of recorded experience is properly applicable to his own circumstances and character."[26] There is no step in this process that is completely autonomous or isolated from social forces; to say so would be to endorse the caricature of the "radical individual."

At the same time, however, at every step there's an opportunity—and a responsibility—for the individual to assert her autonomy and steer her own identity in the direction of the person she wants to become. It's a responsibility because, in Kant's ethics, autonomy not only describes our capacity for independent choice, but also makes this a requirement. We can't simply say that someone "made us" do something, whether taking an action or adopting a taste, unless there was coercion or deceit involved (in which case we were used as tools or means to another's end). We have to take responsibility for our choices insofar as they're our responses to incentives and reasons, regardless of the degree of social influence involved.[27]

This sense of taking responsibility for becoming the person you want to be, or feel you should be, is essential to the concept of the individual I'm arguing for here, and it has precedents in several areas of philosophy. Kantian philosopher Christine Korsgaard, whom we first met at the end of the last chapter, uses the term "self-constitution" to refer to how our choices constantly define and refine the persons we are—our *character*—which then helps determine the choices we make, and so on. It's an ongoing circular process in which we make choices and those choices "make" us in return, reflecting and reinforcing our basic character as decision-makers. As Korsgaard writes, "to be a person is to be constantly engaged in making yourself into that person" by making choices that flow from your moral character and return to it to help shape it for future choices.[28] If you've ever considered an action you're not sure about, such as lying about your age to be eligible for an award, you may have thought to yourself, "is this who I am?" or "is this the person I want to be?" We often feel torn when confronted with ethically difficult choices, but "in the course of this process, of falling apart and pulling yourself back together," as Korsgaard puts it, "you create something new, you constitute something new: yourself."[29] Just as a muscle must be torn down to grow stronger, moral conflict makes our character stronger as well through the process of spurring reflection on how we are and who we want to be—and making a choice that leads us there.[30]

This is an insight of *existentialism* as well, a school of philosophy that emphasizes the freedom and responsibility of individuals to decide for themselves who they are and what they are going to do with their lives. Existentialists such as Jean-Paul Sartre and Simone de Beauvoir argued that individuals must be *authentic* and not just follow the crowd, letting others define us rather than defining ourselves.[31] One of Sartre's most famous quotes is that "existence precedes essence," by which he meant that our meaning, purpose, or function as individuals is not determined at birth, but is assigned to us, either by others or by ourselves.[32] The existentialist would say we need to reject the roles others try to impose on us and instead act on the ability, the responsibility—and yes, the burden—to determine our own essence. This is not to deny the importance of the place in the world we are born into, such as our socio-economic position, race, and sex, but stresses the need to work within them to craft our own selves (such as when transgender individuals decide their gender identity does not correspond to the sex "assigned" to them biologically). As philosopher Skye Cleary wrote, "we shouldn't use our biology or history as excuses not to act. The existential goal is to be an agent, to take control over our life, actively transcending the facts of our existence by pursuing self-chosen goals."[33] The existentialists' sense of authenticity emphasizes the responsibility we have by virtue of autonomy in Kant's sense. If Korsgaard is correct in saying that our choices help define who we are, then we must make all of our choices in the spirit of autonomy or authenticity to preserve our idea of who we want to be.[34]

An important aspect of authenticity is that even though it means not submitting to anyone else's (or society's) idea of who we should be, it doesn't mean that we must always defy authority or social pressure. A rigid refusal to conform to social expectations is actually conformist in the sense that we're letting other people determine our choices. For example, if you wear black every time your roommate wears white and vice versa, you're being different from him, but you're not making your own decisions. What authenticity does mean, however, is that we must reflect upon and endorse the recommendations of others before accepting them, just as we should do when Amazon or Netflix recommends a movie. It's fine to have role models or mentors that we look up to, take advice from, and even emulate, as long as we don't follow their behavior unquestioningly. It's fine to watch the same blood-soaked period drama on HBO that all of your coworkers are watching, as long as you make the decision to watch it in our own interests—interests that may even include being accepted by your coworkers, which are completely valid in certain contexts. The important thing is that you make the choice in your own interests, even when those interests are conformist in nature, and not in blind reliance on what others want you to do; as Mill wrote, "he who lets the world, or his own portion of it, choose his plan of life for him, has no need of any other faculty than the ape-like one of imitation."[35]

This becomes especially crucial when the "others" telling you to do something are in a position of authority over you, whether formal (your boss or your parents, when you're young or even not so young) or informal (an expert such as a doctor, lawyer, or teacher), or even impersonal (social norms, institutions, or even "the system" as a whole). Even when someone with legitimate authority over you tells you to do something, the autonomous or authentic individual has a responsibility to determine whether he or she is comfortable morally with it. This isn't relevant to most ordinary work tasks, such as serving coffee, filing a motion in court, or choreographing a ballet; it arises more often when ethical lines are crossed, such as when you are told to cheat a customer, fudge numbers on a report, or ignore sexual harassment that you have witnessed (or endured). Most of us know these things are wrong, but we don't always know how to react in these cases—and when your job may be on the line, it is reasonable to be hesitant to stand up to your boss. It's easy for someone like me to say "you must always do the right thing," but it's much harder to do in real life with many other circumstances to consider. The least that an autonomous person can do is to make a conscious decision one way or the other without automatically giving in to authority.

Nonetheless, we can point to some evidence that people on average are too compliant and not authentic or autonomous enough, drawn from famous and alarming studies from psychology (falling under the general term of *deindividuation*). In his conformity experiments, psychologist Solomon Asch showed that people are all too willing to go along with popular opinion even when it is clearly wrong. In one version, a group of people—one test subject and a number of "confederates" who are cooperating in the experiment—are presented with a simple problem such as comparing lengths of different lines printed on a card. After the confederates gave the wrong answer (by design), the test subject gave the same obviously incorrect answer a third of the time.[36] People who feel pressure to conform their stated opinions to those of the group—especially without being compelled or urged by anyone—are being inauthentic and conforming to group opinion, even when they *know* the prevailing "opinion" is factually incorrect.

Other, more disturbing studies demonstrated human beings' willingness, not simply to conform to the prevailing opinion, but actually to inflict pain on each other when commanded to by an informal authority figure. In his famous obedience experiments, psychologist Stanley Milgram showed that test subjects were all too willing to administer increasingly powerful electric shocks to another person when the director of the experiment told them to. While the shocks were faked and the "victim" was in on the ruse, almost two-thirds of test subjects drove the shocks all the way to "lethal" or "XXX" levels, and *all* subjects delivered shocks sufficient to cause (simulated) visible pain.[37] In another study, known as the "Stanford prison experiments," psychologist Philip Zimbardo housed a group of students in a fake prison, randomly divided them into "prisoners" and "guards," and then monitored their behavior. According to the standard interpretation of events, within 24 hours the "guards" began abusing the "prisoners," simply based on the roles they were assigned in the study.[38]

These studies are disturbing for many reasons, but the one most relevant to our discussion is that these test subjects so easily complied with orders from those with no formal authority over them, or simply the suggestion of behavior based on an assigned role. And this behavior is not only found in experiments. For example, the 2012 film *Compliance*, written and directed by Craig Zobel, dramatizes the real-life story of a man who called into fast-food restaurants in the Midwest, pretending to be a police officer, and proceeded to subject the managers and other employees to increasingly perverse demands, including strip searches and sexual assault.[39] As a blogger for *Psychology Today*, I was invited to a screening of the film, which was very effective at eliciting discomfort from its audience (more than a few of whom walked out in the middle). Afterward, Zobel and cast discussed the film with the audience, and I was struck by the moderator's introduction, which spoke to the "fact" that we are all raised to be obedient and compliant, with much of the audience nodding in agreement.

Even if few of us will ever encounter a situation as extreme as the one in the movie or in the experiments surveyed above, this inculcation of obedience and compliance, if true, is just as disturbing given the less dramatic but more frequent moral dilemmas we encounter in our ordinary lives. Ideally, the authentic or autonomous person reflectively endorses all of her preferences and choices to make sure they align with who she is and who she wants to be. This is line with Kant's sense of autonomy, in that we should never make decisions in blind obedience to either external authority *or* our own wants or desires, and also existentialists' sense of authenticity, in terms of creating the self we want to be. (One reason I like Korsgaard's idea of self-constitution is that it highlights the connection between these two ideas brilliantly.) We have a duty to comply with authority only if the authority is legitimate *and* if the request itself is valid (not wrongful); otherwise, our obligation is to resist (within the bounds of personal safety and the safety of others).[40]

Our responsibility to craft who we are also extends to the roles we take on, the groups we identify with, and how we behave and adopt the norms and expectations of both. Each of us inhabits a number of roles in our lives: parent, friend, mentor, employee, supervisor, leader, coach, and so on. We also have specific roles within each of these categories: Two parents may play different roles in their child's life, spouses or partners have different responsibilities within their relationship, and each worker or manager in a company has a different part to play in its successful operation. Many of us identify strongly with these roles, accepting them as part of who we are (our identities); it is not uncommon to hear someone say that they don't know who they would be if they weren't a mother, a teacher, a soldier, or whatever role they feel describes them best.

As important as our roles and group affiliations are, the authentic person does not automatically absorb them into her essence or identity. Of course, we do accept casual roles all the time that we don't consider part of our identities, such as being chosen as the parent to bring snacks to their kids' softball game this week.[41] For the roles and affiliations we take more seriously as part of who we are, the authentic person consciously chooses to vest herself in them and integrate them into her concept of herself. As Korsgaard writes,

> The task of self-constitution involves finding some roles and fulfilling them with integrity and dedication. It also involves integrating those roles into a single identity, into a coherent life. People are more or less successful at constituting their identities as unified agents, and a good action is one that does this well. It is one that both *achieves* and *springs* from the integrity of the person who performs it.[42]

By actively endorsing our roles and affiliations, we make them part of who we are, rather than simply an activity we engage in (even if sincerely and wholeheartedly). Someone may feel he identifies, in this strong sense, with being a father but not with his job, while someone else may identify with her role as a government leader but not as an aunt to her nephews. Each of these persons has chosen which roles are part of who they are and which are not, in the process of constructing their identities as individuals in the world.

Some would argue that our various roles comprise our identities in whole: In other words, if Bob is a father, teacher, and amateur bowler, these roles wholly determine who he is. But each individual plays an important part in determining not only what roles he will adopt but also how deeply he identifies with them, and they never define him completely. Economic sociologist Mark Granovetter recognizes this: In the context of both the atomistic view of the individual and the completely "socialized" one, he writes that we should avoid "the theoretical extremes of under- and oversocialized conceptions. Actors do not behave or decide as atoms outside a social context, nor do they adhere slavishly to a script written for them by the particular intersection of social categories that they happen to occupy."[43] Perhaps, Bob feels being a father is an important part of who he is—he identifies strongly with being a father and can't imagine life without being one—while bowling is simply a pastime to him, a way to keep in touch with old friends. It is Bob's choice which roles he embraces and to what extent, and how much those roles help determine his choices and actions. Even those roles he embraces strongly do not make Bob who he is, but rather, it is Bob who chooses to embrace those roles—and perhaps discard them later in his life, remaining, as always, Bob.

Even though we don't consciously think of our various roles as choices, more often taking them for granted, at bottom they *are* choices, expressions of our autonomy, and yet more ways in which we define who we are as individuals in the context of our various social ties. Thinking of our roles this way does not deny or diminish the value of these social ties; it simply affirms that we choose, as individuals, which roles and identities to embrace. By emphasizing that we endorse our social ties and links, we affirm their role in our lives as determined *by* us, rather than something we simply accept when they are imposed *on* us. By making our social environment an active, chosen part of our lives, we are highlighting its importance rather than diminishing it.

This idea of identifying with roles can be taken too far, though, especially when that identification dominates one's sense of individuality and uniqueness. This has become apparent in several ways in recent years. One is the rise of identity politics, in which individuals are increasingly likely to identify themselves strongly with groups based on similar race, ethnicity, gender, sexual orientation, or religion. Often, individuals identify closely with such groups out of solidarity or protection, because the characteristics or statuses they share are marginalized or under attack from the majority or mainstream, such as racial minorities or LGBTQ individuals. Of course, there is tremendous value in joining together in support and activism with those who share similar experiences of discrimination and oppression, and the emphasis on intersectionality—that issues such as race, class, gender, and sexual orientation are not distinct but rather interact in various ways— ideally can provide further solidarity among marginalized groups.[44]

Where this can become problematic, however, is when that group association takes precedence over other aspects of one's self, and a person delegates all political autonomy to that group, whether on their own initiative or in response to pressure from the group itself. The latter can take the form of African Americans being called "Uncle Toms" for appearing to side with whites on divisive racial issues, pro-life women having their feminism (and sometimes their very womanhood) questioned by pro-choice women, or members of the Log Cabin Republicans being criticized by other gays and lesbians for their conservative views on other matters. Just because a person chooses to identify and ally with others with whom she shares experiences and struggles does not imply that she must adopt and promote every position held by the majority within this group; to do so violates the external aspect of Kant's autonomy and compromises one's authenticity as a self-defined individual. Ideally, individuals would feel comfortable expressing their identities in terms of many aspects, including identification with groups who share their race, gender, and sexual orientation, as well as the myriad other aspects that make them unique, without feeling pressure to conform to one vision of what any particular group wants them to be.[45]

The danger of subordinating one's identity to a group can also be seen in the rise of populist movements such as those that have spread across Europe, the UK, and the USA in recent years. Like other terms that are often used as accusations rather than identification (such as "neoliberal"), populism can be difficult to nail down; in their short book on the topic, political scientists Cas Muddle and Cristóbal Rovira Kaltwasser define it as "a thin-centered ideology that considers society to be ultimately separated into two homogeneous and antagonistic camps, 'the pure people' versus 'the corrupt elite,' and which argues that politics should be an expression of the *volonté générale* (general will) of the people."[46] We see this especially in far-right versions of populism: Even though they are often opposed to the rights of minorities more likely to engage in identity politics, the populists themselves are often focused on national identity or race as well (although typically the majority nationality or race).

Whatever their focus, modern populists show unquestioning devotion to a mass political movement, one in which individual opinion is sublimated to the whole. Even though a person may be drawn into such a movement because it seems to serve his interests or confirm his beliefs, a fervor often takes over in which devotion to the cause itself, or the central figure in it, seems to overwhelm the ideas and principles that drew people into it in the first place. This is most evident when, after a certain degree of success of the movement, its leaders begin to betray promises made to their supporters but do not lose that support because by that point the movement has become about the leaders themselves and their success rather than the people's interests the leaders promised to promote. When individuals concede their opinions and interests to a movement such as this, they are also behaving inauthentically, letting groups to which they belong —or their leaders, to whom they have promised or pledged loyalty—determine their actions without sufficient reflection and endorsement.[47]

While our usual conceptions of identity politics (on the left) and nationalist populism (on the right) seem diametrically opposed on many grounds, what they share—especially in terms of the argument I'm making here—is that, when taken too far, they both represent individuals sacrificing some degree of their autonomy or authenticity to others. As we recognized at the beginning of this chapter, it's in our social nature to gather in groups, and it's natural to gather with other people with whom we share interests, opinions, and traits. This becomes even more beneficial when banding together promotes group survival, especially from other groups who may be more numerous and powerful and represent a threat (whether real or imagined). As I've maintained throughout this book, however, we can collect in groups without sacrificing our individuality; we can agree to cooperate with shared plans and pursue political goals without signing away our autonomy.

A similar sacrifice of autonomy and authenticity can be seen in the tendencies of so many of us to compare how well we are doing with our neighbors, friends, colleagues, or other peer groups. "Keeping up with Joneses" is such a well-known phenomenon that we take for granted that we do it, and we don't even question whether it misses the point of how we see ourselves and our well-being. In fact, our relative standing vis-à-vis our peers is all too often a component of our subjective well-being, which is included in researchers' measurements of happiness that we discussed earlier. David Brooks goes so far as to say that "all human beings go through life with a fully operational status sonar. We send out continual waves of status measurements and receive a stream of positive or negative feedback signals that cumulatively define our place in society" and that this "isn't even a conscious process most of the time" but "just the hedonic tone of existence."[48] Even though it may be a psychological fact that ranking our status among others is important to our sense of well-being, it's inauthentic because it ties our sense of self to how others are doing. As philosopher Alain de Botton writes in his book *Status Anxiety*, "if our position on the ladder is of such concern, it is because our self-conception is so dependent on what others make of us," as opposed to what we make of ourselves.[49]

In *The Averaged American*, historian Sarah Igo discusses the rise in the popularity of surveys and polls—the "original" quantification, if you will—and attributes it not only to the needs of business and government, but also to the American people's growing desire to see how they fit into the rest of society and how they compare to the "average" person in income, political opinion, and, in the case of the famous Kinsey studies, sexual behavior. By making us aware of our diversity on all of these dimensions—while, at the same time, obscuring our diversity in terms of race and religion—this obsession with comparison only makes us more conformist, with many people trying to "be" the average rather than be exceptional or simply unique.[50] According to Igo, surveys and polls did not reflect American society so much as they *made* American society, crafting our image of it as well as promoting conformity within it. "The kind of public created by the dissemination of such knowledge about itself," she wrote, "was at once highly intrusive and completely anonymous, self-scrutinizing and other-directed, familiar and impersonal. In a word, it was the backdrop for some of the peculiar tensions of life in a 'mass' society: between being 'oneself' and being known as a member of a group, between being an individual and being a statistic."[51]

Ideally, this impulse to compare and compete with our peers that runs counter to our autonomy and authenticity should be seen as a cognitive bias to be corrected, not a "rational" preference to be promoted, served, and satisfied, in the same sense that we should try to overcome our unconscious biases with regard to race and gender. While this drive to stay ahead of the pack may have served our distant evolutionary ancestors well, in the modern day the rat race never ends and no one ever wins—except the person who drops out to follow her own path and any others who join her in the spirit of cooperation rather than competition.

In summary, while social forces undeniably affect who we are, what we like, and what we do, our capacity for autonomous choice allows us—and demands of us—that we endorse all of these influences in the goal of constructing our authentic selves, the person we want to be and feel we should be. As sociologist Peter Callero writes in his book *The Myth of Individualism*, "we are both free to act on our choices *and*, at the same time, very powerful social forces shape us."[52] The radical individualism that Callero, Brooks, and others argue against—the isolated, antisocial, self-reliant lone wolf—may be an empirical reality in some unfortunate cases but is not representative of what the individual *must* be. In the more nuanced and elaborate picture I've drawn here, the individual acknowledges the influences of the world around them on their preferences, beliefs, and position in society and makes decisions within that context, autonomously and authentically, to reinforce the person they choose to be.

…Social in Orientation

There is another, equally important but more direct way in which the more nuanced conception of the individual is social: how the individual acts through his or her actions or choices. Just as the individual is free to accept social influences into her personal identity, she can also choose as an individual, autonomously and authentically, to act in the interests of others in society. Simply asserting that a person has autonomy does not imply that she will use that autonomy solely in her own self-interest. This is yet another aspect of the exceedingly narrow conception of the individual that leads some to question our moral competence as persons.

Ironically, perhaps, we can turn to many of the same fields of science that prompted questions about the cognitive competence of the individual to support the position that the individual is not always out for his or her own self-interest. As we have seen, psychologists, neuroscientists, and evolutionary biologists—and even economists—have provided evidence and arguments that human beings evolved to be altruistic, at least in certain situations and toward certain groups.[53] In the current day, countless experiments with people (usually college students) playing simple economic games have shown that people have some innate sense of fairness when distributing financial gains (at least when they are not earned).[54]

Evolved moral sentiments are great for showing that some sense of ethical behavior comes naturally to human beings, but we should consider this a bare minimum—and in fact, this is what we often see in children, where claims of "that is not fair" while playing are common and loud while displaying very little positive social behavior. (See also: adults.) Ideally, as children mature, they develop more of a conscious, reflective sense of morality in which they recognize the importance and interests of the people they know and eventually those of people around the world whom they may never meet. They absorb moral lessons, directly or not, from many sources, including relatives, teachers, religious leaders, and stories they learn from books, TV, and movies. All these sources provide examples of ethical behavior, often in the form of moral exemplars or role models, people who demonstrate moral character we admire and whom we can emulate.[55]

However we acquire our sense of right and wrong or good and bad, we carry it into every decision-making context that evokes it. Only a psychopath goes through life with no care whatsoever for other people; the rest of us take the interests of others into account to some extent in most of the decisions we make, whether or not our final choices always reflect that. We may not articulate it like a philosopher would, of course, but we "know" when our actions have a negative impact of others. We may think of ethical situations in terms of fairness, justice, respect, or harm—all of which have formal analogues in moral philosophy, which at the end of the day describes commonsense morality rather than crafts it from blank clay.

Immanuel Kant, in particular, explicitly saw his moral philosophy as representing and formalizing the ordinary moral thinking of average people. Although students in introductory philosophy courses who struggle to grasp its nuances may disagree, Kant believed that the categorical imperative "agrees completely" with "the ordinary reason of mankind in its practical judgments... To be sure, such reason does not think of this principle abstractly in its universal form, but does always have it actually in view and does use it as the standard of judgment."[56] This is true especially if you avoid the formalisms of the categorical imperative itself and focus on the moral concepts at its heart: the equal dignity of all persons and the respect and reciprocal treatment it demands. From this, he derives the universalization formula for the categorical imperative, which asks us to consider what would happen if everyone were free to do what we are thinking of doing, and the formula of respect, which, as we have seen, demands that persons treat each other as valuable ends in themselves and never simply as means to their own ends.[57]

You may recall from earlier in this chapter that the categorical imperative and the concept of dignity itself are both derived from autonomy, which to Kant is both a capacity for independent decision-making—which we discussed at length in the previous section—and a responsibility *to use it well*. Not only must we make moral decisions regardless of external pressure or internal desire, but we must also make them according to "the moral law," preferably with the assistance of the categorical imperative, to result in ethical decisions regarding other persons as well as ourselves. Put more generally, despite the individualistic orientation of Kant's ethics, his conception of autonomy does not equal a license to be a libertine, but instead implies a responsibility to be a moral person.

You will likely be surprised to learn that Kant has developed somewhat of a reputation as a harsh and demanding ethicist, mainly due to a widespread misunderstanding of the duties we can derive from the categorical imperative and how strictly they bind our action.[58] Although this aspect of his ethics is exaggerated, his moral philosophy *is* demanding in terms of respect and concern for other persons, regardless of exactly how we might put these attitudes into action in particular situations. Kant is also widely regarded as favoring individualism over social concerns; as philosopher Robert Louden explains, "Kant is often portrayed as an extreme moral individualist, one who holds that each moral agent is an end in itself, a discrete individual owed respect for its autonomy, an autonomy that is safeguarded by inviolable rights."[59] While this much is accurate, what is left out of this statement is that *every* individual is to be considered this way by *every* other, which generates our duties to each other as well as to ourselves.

It is Kant's emphasis on duty that gives him his reputation as harsh and rigid, although these are undeserved as well. While Kant maintained that we must always do the right thing, as demanded by autonomy and out of respect for human dignity, determining the right thing to do in any given situation is much more difficult. The duties that come from the categorical imperative are nothing more than guidelines, such as "do not lie" or "help others," which do not give us precise instructions on what we need to do to be moral. We shouldn't lie, of course, but neither do we have to be completely forthright: When asked a direct question, we can change the topic, respond with another question, or simply say nothing. What we must not do is lie, which would treat the other person simply as a means to our ends by not letting them in on the deception (which would defeat the purpose of the lie). By the same token, when we see an opportunity to help someone, we're free to choose what we do to help, how much we do to help, or if we even help at all. Literally, all the categorical imperative tells us to do is "do not be indifferent to the suffering of others," which merely demands an attitude of helpfulness that we should put into action when we can. It is up to each of us to decide whether we can be of help of certain situations: Bending over to pick up a dropped book would normally be expected, but for most of us, running into a burning building to save a child would not be.

This highlights the role of *judgment* in Kant's ethics, which balances three important factors: the role of duties as guidelines to doing the right thing, the fact that duties often conflict, and, when they do, the difficulty of determining which duty takes precedence. For example, suppose you have made a promise to help your best friend move on Saturday, but on Friday evening your mother asks you to see her favorite movie (and mine!), *Singin' in the Rain*, with her at a special exclusive screening at the local theater—at the same time Saturday that your best friend has booked her moving van. You feel an obligation to both, but you can't fulfill them both; you have to choose one obligation and break the other. On this topic, Kant didn't say much, only that your singular duty depends on which obligation has the "stronger ground," a determination that, he implied, can be made only by using your judgment.[60] You have different obligations to both your mother and best friend, so you need to decide—or judge—which is more important (or has the "stronger ground"). For some, it would be their mother by default, but not for all. Perhaps you made the promise to your best friend months ago, and you saw *Singin' in the Rain* with your mother last time it was shown in the theater, so your best friend wins out. Or maybe there is some other consideration about the grounds of the two obligations that can help you decide which one will be your duty to act on.

As this example shows, there's no rule or formula to make judgment simpler. As Kant wrote, "though understanding is capable of being instructed… judgment is a peculiar talent which can be practiced only, and cannot be taught. It is the specific quality of so-called mother-wit; and its lack no school can make good."[61] Each of us develops a moral sense or intuition, a feeling of right and wrong, informed by making ethical decisions throughout our life, which helps us make judgment calls in cases of conflicting obligations. Because every person's experiences and choices are different, each person has his or her own unique faculty of judgment. In our example, some people will decide to help their best friend move, while others will choose to go with their mother to see the best movie ever made.[62] Furthermore, each individual who decides to help their best friend move made that decision for their own unique reasons, as did each individual who chose to go to the movie with their mom, in the same way that each individual makes choices in general in their own unique interests.

In this way, a focus on Kantian autonomy allows individuals to craft their own unique ethical identities or moral characters through the way they choose to balance obligations (in the process of self-constitution), while also ensuring that they act with respect and care toward others based on their equal dignity and autonomy. Because every individual has dignity, we must never take actions that could affect other people without first considering the impact on them, in terms of both harm and respect. Avoiding harm may be the more obvious ethical demand, but maintaining respect is also essential and reflects the importance of dignity. This element gives Kant's ethics a unique flavor, forbidding acts of deception and coercion that may end up helping people while denying them a full role in the decision-making process, including lies told "for a person's own good" as well as paternalistic government policies such as nudges. Even acts of kindness must be tempered to avoid offense; as Kant wrote, "since the favor we do implies that his well-being depends on our generosity, and this humbles him, it is our duty to behave as if our help is either merely what is due him or but a slight service of love, and to spare him humiliation and maintain his respect for himself."[63] In modern times, we might say "no big deal" or "no problem" to convey the same token of respect while acting out of kindness and altruism, which emphasizes the importance of both.

Conclusion

It is the dual nature of autonomy in Kant's terms that lies at the core of my phrase "individual in essence, social in orientation." Kant's autonomy provides a firm basis for the unique and distinct nature of each individual, who must not only determine her own choices and actions but is also charged with developing the moral sense described by the categorical imperative—which is then used to make choices that reflect respect and concern for other persons. This reinforces the point that emphasizing our individuality does not imply that our choices will be selfish or antisocial. (And it gave me a chance to talk about my favorite philosopher, which I simply Kant resist.)

This also leads us back to my earlier point about individuals and their relationship to each other and society. As we saw, critics of the individual often construct a straw man of an isolated and selfish person, not interacting with other people and believing he can do everything for himself, "a self-made man" that needs no one else and helps no one else. As with most things, the real picture is much more nuanced. The individual properly considered does not regard herself as a force of one, but acknowledges her dependence *and* impact on those around her. She takes responsibility for her contribution to her accomplishments—for better or for worse—while also giving credit to others who also contributed to it (as well as the element of luck). Again, we can acknowledge that not everyone does this; some take more credit than they deserve, while others are eager to give to others credit that is owed to them. But there is nothing in the concept of the individual that denies the cooperative nature of most human endeavors or the recognition of each individual's unique and invaluable contribution to them.

Despite evidence of our evolved moral sentiments as well as our conscious adoption of ethical standards, critics maintain that the individual is inherently selfish and antisocial. Criticism such as this serves to question the *moral competency* of individuals who, after being reduced to simple motives of pure selfishness, come to resemble ethical cretins. This not only serves to diminish the status of the individual within society, but also serves to justify intervention by the state to incite them to behave kindly (if not respectfully) toward others.[64] By painting the individual into one corner, critics can then argue that the only solution is to go to the other corner, where institutional pressure and control take the place of the moral sense that their caricature of the individual lacks. People are selfish, the story goes, so the state must force them to be kind. Individual compassion is rendered a myth, only to be replaced by the compassion of the state, with no acknowledgment of a middle ground (or, more to the point, mistaken assumptions to begin with).[65]

This is a direct consequence of an insultingly reductionist conception of the individual and her decision-making processes that can only imagine self-interested behavior, joined with an equally simplistic and naive idea of the state in which noble bureaucrats selflessly serve the public good and correct for the moral incompetence of the unenlightened citizenry. But both of these notions are absurd: Citizens are not devils, and public servants are not saints. Rather, they are all human beings, able to act altruistically as well as selfishly, making independent choices for better or for worse in light of the myriad institutional and societal influences acting on them. As we have seen, individuals often set their own self-interest aside in pursuit of fairness and the well-being of others, without any coercion from our betters looking to adjust their behavior while assuming that we're little more than broken machines as described in an earlier chapter. It all comes back to an overly simplified conception of who we are as individuals and what we are capable of. Where this conception sees individuals as hopelessly flawed, irrational, and selfish decision-makers, we actually make decisions in our complex, multifaceted, and subjective interests which include concern and respect for other people as well as ourselves—and to judge these decisions to be wrong, prudentially or ethically, based on a mischaracterization of our capacities themselves or the choices we make, is the height of presumption and insult.

Not only does such criticism cast into doubt the moral competence of the individual, but it also works to obscure and minimize the contribution made to society by individuals in favor of a collectivist notion of responsibility, again replacing one extreme view with another. It is no contradiction to recognize that individuals do nothing completely on their own and at the same time that they are responsible for some of what they accomplish. There is room between "I built this all by myself" and "you didn't build that," and to deny this is not only a tremendous disincentive for individual effort, to the extent that people like to receive credit for their work (not only out of vanity or pride but also to help gain advancement in their fields), but it also represents a failure to respect the valuable contribution made by those who make choices and take action, namely individuals, whether acting alone or in groups. No individual is self-reliant, but the individual's initiative is nonetheless essential. By the same token, no individual deserves sole credit for achievements that built on or relied on the work of others, but neither is all credit to be distributed equally as a rule—as anybody who has collaborated on a group project knows full well.

Once again, this is not a choice of one or the other. We must resist such false dichotomies; this is not a competition that needs to be won by the side with the better arguments. There need be no disagreement here: Individuals are capable of doing great things, especially when they work together. But they work together *as individuals.* By saying this, I'm not questioning the value of cooperation. I'm only clarifying *who* is doing the cooperating. A team is a group of individuals, working toward a common goal by pooling their unique perspectives, talents, and faculties of judgment. We can usually accomplish more by working together than going at it alone, but this need not obscure the fact that the "we" is made up of many "I"s. The popular adage says there is no "I" in "team," but the truth is that a team is nothing but "I"s. Rather than diminishing the accomplishments of teams, this makes them all the more admirable, stressing that they are the coordinated efforts of many minds rather than one. Anyone who has run a team, whether in a committee room, a battlefield, or a sports field, knows that it involves dealing with individuals that must be brought together—and if this can be done well, anything is possible. But it must be done.

Finally, underlying this artificial conflict between the individual and society, we find a shift, enabled by a distorted and simplistic view of the individual, towards a collectivist mindset in which the concerns of the individual are subordinated to those of the whole. By depicting the individual as morally incompetent, especially when it comes to promoting the well-being of others, it falls to another party or authority to safeguard the well-being of all. As we have seen, a natural candidate would seem to be the state, which is often seen as a benevolent counterpoint to the selfish actions of individuals, who are understood not only to make poor decisions in their own interests (as we saw in the last two chapters) but also to be incapable of thinking of anyone else. Even those who doubt the ability of the state to do this effectively may nonetheless endorse the promotion of aggregate well-being or utility based in part on the diminution of the individual due to the trends I've described here. We turn to that in the next chapter, in which we argue for a restoration of respect for the individual and the political vision that follows.

Notes

1. Aristotle, *Politics*, 350 BCE, translated by Benjamin Jowett, Book I, 1253a, available at http://classics.mit.edu/Aristotle/politics.1.one.html.
2. Immanuel Kant, "Idea for a Universal History with a Cosmopolitan Intent," in *Perpetual Peace and Other Essays*, translated by Ted Humphrey (Indianapolis, IN: Hackett Publishing Company, 1983), pp. 29–40 at pp. 31–32. He echoes this elsewhere; for instance, he wrote that "the human being is a being meant for society (though he is also an unsociable one)" (*The Metaphysics of Morals*, translated and edited by Mary J. Gregor, Cambridge: Cambridge University Press, 1797/1996, p. 471).
3. Jean-Paul Sartre, *No Exit and Three Other Plays* (New York: Vintage International, 1989), p. 45.
4. For instance, see Robert Wright, *The Moral Animal: Evolutionary Psychology and Everyday Life* (New York: Vintage, 1994), especially parts 2 and 3; Samuel Bowles and Herbert Gintis, *A Cooperative Species: Human Reciprocity and Its Evolution* (Princeton, NJ: Princeton University Press, 2011); Matthew D. Lieberman, *Social: Why Our Brains Are Wired to Connect* (New York: Broadway Books, 2014).
5. For popular overviews, see Laura Geggel, "How Racism Persists: Unconscious Bias May Play a Role," *Live Science*, July 8, 2016, at http://www.livescience.com/55337-unconscious-racial-bias.html; Princess Ojiaku, "Is everybody a racist?", *Aeon*, March 21, 2016, at https://aeon.co/essays/unconscious-racism-is-pervasive-starts-early-and-can-be-deadly. A particularly influential paper is Elizabeth A. Phelps et al, "Performance on Indirect Measures of Race Evaluation Predicts Amygdala Activation," *Journal of Cognitive Neuroscience* 12(2000): 729–738; see also the exchange involving Troy Duster, Lincoln Quillian, and Philip E. Tetlock and Gregory Mitchell in the March 2008 issue of *Social Psychology Quarterly*.

6. For an argument that this problem merits more direct intervention, see Ingmar Persson and Julian Savulescu, "Moral Hard-Wiring and BIoenhancement," *Bioethics* 31(2017): 286–295.
7. Stephen Bachelor, *Alone with Others: An Existential Approach to Buddhism* (New York: Grove Press, 1983).
8. A classic in this genre is Robert D. Putnam, *Bowling Alone: The Collapse and Revival of American Community* (New York: Touchstone, 2001); columnist David Brooks, who we'll discuss soon, also often writes about the decline in civic participation and faith in institutions. For a perspective from psychology and neuroscience, see Lieberman, *Social*. Specifically, on the decline in the number of close friends, see Jeanna Bryner, "Close Friends Less Common Today, Study Finds," *Live Science*, November 4, 2011, at http://www.livescience.com/16879-close-friends-decrease-today.html, reporting on Matthew E. Brashears, "Small networks and high isolation?: A re-examination of American discussion networks," *Social Networks* 33(2010): 331-341 (profiled widely in the popular press at the time). On the growing problem of toxic loneliness, see Judith Shulevitz, "The Lethality of Loneliness," *New Republic*, May 13, 2013, at https://newrepublic.com/article/113176/science-loneliness-how-isolation-can-kill-you, and Katie Hafner, "Researchers Confront on Epidemic of Loneliness," *The New York Times*, September 5, 2016, at https://www.nytimes.com/2016/09/06/health/lonliness-aging-health-effects.html.
9. Sociologist Peter L. Callero begins his book *The Myth of Individualism* with the story of Ted Kaczynski, the famous Unabomber, as an example of radical individualism (see *The Myth of Individualism: How Social Forces Shape Our Lives*, 2nd ed., Lanham, MD: Rowman & Littlefield, 2013, pp. 11–16).
10. David Brooks, *The Social Animal: The Hidden Sources of Love, Character, and Achievement*, rev. ed. (New York: Random House, 2012).
11. David Brooks, "It's Not About You," *The New York Times*, May 30, 2011, at http://www.nytimes.com/2011/05/31/opinion/31brooks.html, on which I commented in "David Brooks' false dichotomy regarding autonomy and sociality," *Economics and Ethics*, June 7, 2011, at http://www.economicsandethics.org/2011/06/david-brooks-false-dichotomy-regarding-autonomy-and-sociality.html.
12. This also corresponds fairly well to Callero's conception of individualism, especially the aspect of self-reliance; see *Myth of Individualism*, p. 15.
13. For an overview, see John B. Davis and Wilfred Dolfsma, *The Elgar Companion to Social Economics*, 2nd ed (Cheltenham, UK: Edward Elgar, 2015). Economists outside social economics make similar arguments as well; for example, see Virgil Henry Storr, "The Market as a Social Space:

On the Meaningful Extraeconomic Conversations that Can Occur in Markets," *Review of Austrian Economics* 21(2008): 135–150.
14. Mark Granovetter, "Economic Action and Social Structure: The Problem of Embeddedness," in *The Sociology of Economic Life*, edited by Mark Granovetter and Richard Swedberg (Boulder, CO: Westview Press, 1992), pp. 53–81.
15. Brooks, *Social Animal*, pp. 314–315.
16. Ibid., pp. 197–198.
17. Brooks, "It's Not About You."
18. Christine Korsgaard, *Self-Constitution: Agency, Identity, and Integrity* (Oxford: Oxford University Press, 2009).
19. David Brooks, "Freedom Loses One," *The New York Times*, April 1, 2013, at http://www.nytimes.com/2013/04/02/opinion/brooks-freedom-loses-one.html, on which I commented in "David Brooks on same-sex marriage, freedom and individualism in *The New York Times*," *Economics and Ethics*, April 2, 2013, at http://www.economicsandethics.org/2013/04/david-brooks-on-same-sex-marriage-freedom-and-individualism-in-the-new-york-times.html. (We'll have more to say about *Obergefell* in the next chapter.)
20. Some philosophers, such as Andy Clark, argue that we should also include aspects of the physical world, especially tools such as calculators and cell phones, into our conception of mind, in what is known as "embodied cognition" or "the extended mind." See his article "Out of Our Brains," *The New York Times*, December 12, 2010, at https://opinionator.blogs.nytimes.com/2010/12/12/out-of-our-brains/, and his book *Supersizing the Mind: Embodiment, Action, and Cognition Extension* (Oxford: Oxford University Press, 2008). This concept doesn't usually extend to other minds themselves, although this may not be so outlandish if we imagine two minds cooperating on a problem and solving it together using their mutual insights.
21. In all seriousness, with respect to the Vulcan mind meld, see Lieberman, *Social*, Part 3, on our natural capacities to "mindread" to some extent. With respect to the Borg, some philosophers do argue for various theories of *collective* or *plural agency* in which individual decision-making is questioned in favor of some sort of collective choice, ranging from a belief in a "group mind" to merely "shared intentions" between individuals acting together. For more, see Margaret Gilbert, *Living Together: Rationality, Sociality, & Obligation* (Lanham, MD: Rowman & Littlefield, 1996) and Raimo Tuomela, *The Importance of Us: A Philosophical Study of Basic Social Notions* (Stanford, CA: Stanford University Press, 1995).

22. In fact, much of this section builds on concepts introduced in chapter 3 of my book *Kantian Ethics and Economics: Autonomy, Dignity, and Character* (Stanford: Stanford University Press, 2011).
23. See note 41 in chapter 2.
24. See, for instance, Callero, *Myth of Individualism*, chapter 1.
25. Don't get me started.
26. John Stuart Mill, *On Liberty* (London: Walter Scott Pub. Co., 1859), p. 108, available at http://www.gutenberg.org/ebooks/34901.
27. This is not meant as a comment on free will and responsibility in a metaphysical sense; even if our actions and thoughts are ultimately the result of a purely deterministic, physical process, on a conscious level we still react to reasons presented to us.
28. Korsgaard, *Self-Constitution*, p. 43. Another philosopher, Joel Feinberg, emphasizes this same process of character development, writing that "self-creation in the authentic person must be self-*re*-creation, rationally accommodating new experiences and old policies to make greater coherence and flexibility" (*Harm to Self*, Oxford: Oxford University Press, 1986, p. 35).
29. Korsgaard, *Self-Constitution*, p. 214.
30. While Korsgaard is generally a Kantian philosopher, this emphasis on a person's character also reflects the spirit of *virtue ethics*, which focuses on the person rather than the choices she makes. In the way Korsgaard thinks of the person and her actions as constantly reinventing each other, she's showing that the two approaches to ethics—those based on character, such as virtue ethics, and those based on actions, such as utilitarianism and deontology—can be considered two sides of the same coin. (More on the last two approaches in the next chapter.)
31. For an introduction to the breadth of existentialist thought, see Walter Kaufmann (ed.), *Existentialism from Dostoevsky to Sartre*, rev. and exp. ed. (New York: Penguin, 1975) and William Barrett, *Irrational Man: A Study in Existential Philosophy* (New York: Anchor Books, 1958). For more contemporary takes, see William Irwin, *The Free Market Existentialist: Capitalism without Consumerism* (Malden, MA: Wiley Blackwell, 2015); Skye Cleary, *Existentialism and Romantic Love* (New York: Palgrave Macmillan, 2015); and Sarah Bakewell, *At the Existentialist Café: Freedom, Being, and Apricot Cocktails* (New York: Other Press, 2016).
32. Jean-Paul Sartre, *Existentialism*, translated by Bernard Frechtman (New York: Philosophical Library, 1947), p. 15. While Sartre denied any pre-existing "human nature" at birth, this is at odds with modern science; philosopher William Irwin argues, however, that these two views can be reconciled. See Irwin, *Free Market Existentialist*, chapters 4 and 5.

33. Skye Cleary, "Simone de Beauvoir's political philosophy resonates today," *Aeon*, March 10, 2017, at https://aeon.co/ideas/simone-de-beauvoirs-political-philosophy-resonates-today. See, in particular, Beauvior's *The Ethics of Ambiguity* (New York: Philosophical Library, 1947).
34. Kant and the existentialists disagree, however, on who a person *should* be, Kant maintaining that a rational person must follow the moral law and the existentialists being more skeptical about morality in general (especially Nietzsche).
35. Mill, *On Liberty*, p. 109.
36. Solomon E. Asch, "Effects of Group Pressure upon the Modification and Distortion of Judgments," in Harold Guetzkow (ed.), *Groups, Leadership and Men: Research in Human Relations* (Oxford: Carnegie Press, 1951), pp. 177–190.
37. Stanley Milgram, *Obedience to Authority: An Experimental View* (New York: Harper and Row, 1974). On the significant ethical concerns raised by Milgram's experiments, see Gina Perry, *Behind the Shock Machine: The Untold Story of the Notorious Milgram Psychology Experiments* (New York: The New Press, 2013). These experiments and the controversies with them were effectively dramatized in the 2015 film *Experimenter*, directed by Michael Almereyda and starring Peter Sarsgaard as Milgram.
38. Craig Haney, Curtis Banks, and Philip Zimbardo, "Interpersonal Dynamics in a Simulated Prison," *International Journal of Criminology and Penology* 1(1973): 69–97. Many details are available at the Stanford Prison Experiment website, http://www.prisonexp.org/, including a film of the same name, also released in 2015, directed by Kyle Patrick Alvarez and starring Billy Crudup as Zimbardo. Zimbardo discusses his famous experiments in the context of more recent real-life incidents such as Abu Ghraib in *The Lucifer Effect: Understanding How Good People Turn Evil* (New York: Random House, 2007). And yes, like the Milgram studies, Zimbardo's experiment is also very controversial; for example, see Maria Konnikova, "The Real Lesson of the Stanford Prison Experiment," *The New Yorker*, June 12, 2015, at http://www.newyorker.com/science/maria-konnikova/the-real-lesson-of-the-stanford-prison-experiment.
39. On the case that inspired the film, see Andrew Wolfson, "A hoax most cruel: Caller coaxed McDonald's managers into strip-searching a worker," *The Courier-Journal*, October 9, 2005, at http://www.courier-journal.com/story/news/local/2005/10/09/a-hoax-most-cruel-caller-coaxed-mcdonalds-managers-/28936597/.
40. As I was finalizing this chapter, news broke of Dr. David Dao, a man brutally removed from an overbooked United Airlines flight when he refused to give up his seat "voluntarily," to which some responded that he

should have obeyed United's "command" to leave and "he should expected to be beaten" for not complying. (For the initial report of the incident, see Lucas Aulbach, "Video shows man forcibly removed from United flight from Chicago to Louisville," *The Courier-Journal*, April 10, 2017, at http://www.courier-journal.com/story/news/2017/04/10/video-shows-man-forcibly-removed-united-flight-chicago-louisville/100274374/.) There were many other ways United could have dealt with this situation, but having airport security violently remove him from his seat and the plane when he refused to comply was an abhorrent abuse of illegitimate authority, and the responses in support of this dehumanizing act may have been even worse.
41. Oh crap… I'll be right back. Sorry. Keep reading.
42. Korsgaard, *Self-Constitution*, p. 25.
43. Granovetter, "Economic Action and Social Structure," p. 58.
44. Identity politics itself became a very political issue around the 2016 presidential election, usually identified with the left; its critics (chiefly from the right) argue that it distracts from national identity and splinters the public. See, for instance, Mark Lilla, "The End of Identity Liberalism," *The New York Times*, November 18, 2016, at https://www.nytimes.com/2016/11/20/opinion/sunday/the-end-of-identity-liberalism.html. In my view, the issue is more with the impulse to identify too strongly with *any* group, not whether that group is defined narrowly (such as a race or gender) or widely (such as a nationality), and to sacrifice one's autonomy and individualized identity to that group.
45. This is not to deny, of course, that groups have some prerogative to decide who does and does not belong or qualify, and that this conflicts with individuals' desire to self-identify. Consider the struggle of transgendered persons to be accepted into the gender they identify with, or the controversy over Rachel Dolezal, the woman who was born white but identifies as African-American. Despite the differences between these two cases, at their core the issue they share is who gets to define or determine who "merits" inclusion in a specific group, which by its nature must exclude some persons to focus on the similarities between its members (based, for instance, on the existence of shared experiences of oppression, a key distinction between the issue of transgender and transrace).
46. Cas Muddle and Cristóbal Rovira Kaltwasser, *Populism: A Very Short Introduction* (Oxford: Oxford University Press, 2017), p. 6.
47. I thank Shawn Klein for suggesting this connection.
48. Brooks, *Social Animal*, pp. 202–203.
49. Alain de Botton, *Social Anxiety* (New York: Vintage, 2004), p. viii.
50. As John Stuart Mill wrote, "In sober truth, whatever homage may be professed, or even paid, to real or supposed mental superiority, the general

tendency of things throughout the world is to render mediocrity the ascendant power among mankind" (*On Liberty*, p. 123). For a unique perspective on conforming to the norm rather than striving for more, see Tyler Cowen, *The Complacent Class: The Self-Defeating Quest for the American Dream* (New York: St. Martin's Press, 2017).
51. Igo, *Averaged American*, pp. 281–282.
52. Callero, *Myth of Individualism*, p. 9 (emphasis in original).
53. See note 4 above.
54. For example, see Ernst Fehr and Klaus M. Schmidt, "The Economics of Fairness, Reciprocity and Altruism—Experimental Evidence and New Theories," in Serge-Christophe Kolm and Jean Mercier Ythier (eds), *Handbook of the Economics of Giving, Altruism and Reciprocity*, vol. I (Dordrecht: Elsevier, 2006), pp. 615–691.
55. Even superheroes! See my book *The Virtues of Captain America: Modern-Day Lessons on Character from a World War II Superhero* (Hoboken, NJ: Wiley Blackwell, 2014).
56. Immanuel Kant, *Grounding for the Metaphysics of Morals*, translated by James W. Ellington (Indianapolis, IN: Hackett Publishing Company, 1785/1993), pp. 402–404.
57. Ibid, pp. 421 and 429 (respectively). For more on everyone's favorite Kantian concept, see H.J. Paton, *The Categorical Imperative: A Study in Kant's Moral Philosophy* (Philadelphia: University of Pennsylvania Press, 1947).
58. I discuss this misperception in several places, such as my chapter "The Virtues of a Kantian Economics," in Jennifer A. Baker and Mark D. White (eds), *Economics and the Virtues: Building a New Moral Foundation* (Oxford: Oxford University Press, 2016), pp. 94–115.
59. Robert Louden, *Kant's Impure Ethics: From Rational Beings to Human Beings* (Oxford: Oxford University Press, 2000), p. 172.
60. Kant, *Metaphysics of Morals*, p. 224.
61. Kant, *Critique of Pure Reason*, translated by Norman Kemp Smith (New York: St. Martin's Press, 1781/1787/1929), pp. A133/B172. (The A and B correspond to the 1781 and 1787 editions, both of which are combined in most editions.) For a philosopher usually criticized as being too focused on rules, Kant actually rejected them: "Dogmas and formulas, those mechanical instruments for rational use (or rather misuse) of [man's] natural endowments, are the ball and chain of his permanent immaturity" ("An Answer to the Question: What Is Enlightenment?", in *Kant: Political Writings*, 2nd ed., edited by H.S. Reiss and translated by H.B. Nisbet, Cambridge: Cambridge University Press, 1991, pp. 54–60, at pp. 54–55).
62. On this there can be no difference of opinion; it is simply so.
63. Kant, *Metaphysics of Morals*, pp. 448–449.

64. See, for instance, Brooks, *Social Animal*, chapter 20.
65. Contrast this with Irwin, who argues that "the state itself should not be the locus of compassion. Compassion is a virtue to be found in the private sphere, in the individual" (*Free Market Existentialist*, p. 170; see pp. 170–172 more generally on this point).

CHAPTER 5

Balancing the Individual and Society in Law and Politics

Throughout this book, I've tried to explain the reasons underlying the decline in respect for the individual in recent decades. Some of these were scientific or technological, such as the discoveries by psychologists and neuroscientists regarding our thought processes, as well as the advances in predictive power enabled by the explosion in data storage and computing power, all of which suggests that human beings are poor decision-makers, and therefore, others can better make decisions on their behalf. Other signs came from the humanities, portraying individuals in a similarly reductive way that suggests that they cannot make good choices to benefit others (much less themselves). In other words, science and technology imply that individuals are cognitively incompetent, while the humanistic perspective implies that individuals are morally incompetent—both of which lead to a reduction in the value of the individual and, in its place, an elevation of the importance of society as a whole.

This is a significant shift in the balance between the individual and society which, I explain in this chapter, is also reflected in modern politics and law. I argue that this balance has become upset, denying the value of the individual in favor of the "interests" of the whole. Pursuing our valid collective goals as a society should not come at the cost of important individual rights and liberties, which are valued by those on both sides of the political spectrum. Although the left and right often emphasize different rights on the part of the individual, I will argue that they are all essential protections of our unique interests and identities, as codified in the Bill of Rights to the US Constitution and other documents of liberal democracies, and need to be restored to the prominence they deserve as a reflection of our basic dignity as individual persons.

A Little Philosophy to Start Us Off

One natural implication of a decline in respect and consideration for the individual is an increase in emphasis on the group or whole as a thing unto itself. To a certain extent, this is understandable, especially in the context of large-scale political and social issues, in which it's convenient to think of people in the aggregate as a population, nation, or society. Problems arise, however, when the "interests" of the whole are furthered without keeping in mind that the whole is made up of individuals, each with their own unique interests and rights that exist to protect these interests and their choices regarding them. Liberal societies have traditionally protected the rights of the individual, but against the background of the developments surveyed earlier in this book, our respect for those rights and interests is in decline.

We can easily put this conflict into philosophical terms, which is not only interesting in and of itself (right?), but will also help support the political and legal discussion to come. As we have seen several times already in this book, the concern with the aggregate is the characteristic of a *utilitarian* approach to ethics, based on the work of Jeremy Bentham and John Stuart Mill, while individual rights are safeguarded by a *deontological* approach, such as that held by Immanuel Kant (whom we know from earlier chapters, but not necessarily in the context of deontology). Here, we'll recap some of what we said about utilitarianism earlier and then show how deontology can constrain its pursuit of the collective good in the service of individual rights and dignity.

While it has historical precedents going back to ancient times, utilitarianism as we know it today arose in the eighteenth and nineteenth centuries due to the work of Bentham and Mill, who were both social reformers and philosophers.[1] (In those days, that combination was not seen as strange!) In its simplest form, utilitarianism holds that moral evaluation should focus on *utility*, specifically the sum of the utilities of the individual members of society. Utility can be understood in many different ways, from happiness or pleasure (as Bentham maintained) to the satisfaction of preferences or desires (as many modern utilitarian philosophers and economists maintain). In any case, utility is an element of the consequences of an action; for this reason, utilitarianism is a specific version of *consequentialism*, which describes any moral theory based on the outcomes of actions.[2]

More interesting for our purposes is the way that utilitarianism incorporates concern for the individual: Its focus on the simple sum of individual utilities implies that each person's well-being is considered equally by decision-makers. In this sense, utilitarianism treats each person equally, an admirable egalitarian impulse in the day of Bentham and Mill, and sadly, one that would still be considered revolutionary in many places around the world in the current day. Ideally, a utilitarian decision-making process would value the utility of a servant equally with that of a queen, a woman equally with a man, and any person of any race, ethnicity, or religion equally with any other, denying any bias in favor of one group or another for the purposes of moral or political decision-making.

This represents a firm grounding in moral equality that makes utilitarianism very attractive as an ethical system (in addition to what many people see as a common sense and intuitive focus on outcomes). However, merely being treated equally is not necessarily good if everyone is treated equally *poorly*. As we saw earlier, utilitarians' focus on the sum of individual utilities also implies that each person's utility is interchangeable in the total: It matters not whose utility is increased, or whose utility is decreased in order to increase others' by more, as long as the total number goes up. Because of this, utilitarianism ends up treating individuals merely as sources or "locations" of utility that contribute to the total, which then becomes the focus of decision-making.[3] This stands in stark contrast to Kant's position that persons should always be treated as valuable ends in themselves, not simply means to an end that is not their own, and explains the most common criticism of utilitarianism that it endorses "ends justify the means" reasoning, the idea that any method used to achieve a desirable goal is justified by that goal.

We're all taught from an early age, however, that some actions are wrong regardless of whether they lead to good ends. We're taught not to lie, especially not to benefit ourselves, and even in cases of "benevolent lies" that may help the person being lied to. We're also taught not to steal, even if we really want something and even if we are stealing for the good of someone else (as in the famous case of Robin Hood). This way of looking at acts in terms of right and wrong rather than good and bad is representative of *deontology*, which judges actions by their intrinsic nature rather than their outcomes or consequences (as utilitarianism does). Indeed, the contrast between deontology and utilitarianism is often stated in terms of "the right versus the good," as immortalized in the title of a book by W.D. Ross, an important deontologist.[4]

But why are we taught that acts such as lying and stealing are wrong? If it was only that they cause harm—which they often do—then it would come down to simple utilitarian logic. But these actions are not considered merely *bad* (as opposed to good) but also *wrong* (as opposed to right), regardless of whether they cause good or bad outcomes. Different varieties of deontology base this judgment on moral principles, the rights of persons, or duties we have to each other.[5] In a way, these explanations of what makes certain actions wrong beg the question: They do not answer the question so much as shift it, requiring us to ask what it is about moral principles, rights, or duties that make them the basis of right and wrong? Utilitarianism is guilty of this too, however; it holds utility or well-being to be of intrinsic moral value without explaining why. Every moral system has to start somewhere, and what a system declares to be of utmost ethical importance makes that system unique. It may seem obvious to some that pleasure is good and pain is bad, to use Bentham's terms, but it may be just as obvious to others that rights, duties, or principles are important and violating them is wrong. W.D. Ross' deontology embraces this sort of intuition, but another deontologist has a firmer grounding for his theory.

That other deontologist would be none other than Immanuel Kant, whose famous duty-based ethics are often understood to be synonymous with deontology itself. (Sorry, W.D.!) As we saw in earlier chapters, Kant's moral system is grounded in dignity, the incalculable and incomparable worth that rational beings possess by virtue of their capacity for autonomous decision-making. Based on autonomy and dignity, Kant develops his categorical imperative which, when applied to actions people plan to take (or *maxims*), gives us either duties to abstain from those actions (if they fail the categorical imperative "test") or permission to go ahead and do them (if they pass it). For example, lying fails the categorical imperative test, whether based on universalization (if everyone lies whenever they wanted to, no one would believe them, defeating the purpose of lying) or respect (the liar uses the person being lied to merely as a means to the liar's ends without treating the other person as a valuable end as well). The latter version of the categorical imperative puts respect for the dignity of persons front and center, but this is also the basis for the universalization test: The reason why we test maxims by universalizing them at all is because, out of recognition of the equal moral status of all, we must grant others any permissions we grant ourselves.[6]

In general, while utilitarianism incorporates a sense of equal concern for all persons, it fails to respect them as distinct, unique individuals. As a result, there is a constant risk that utilitarian logic will sacrifice the interests for the few for the sake of the many, without adequate consideration of the rights or interests of all. This can actually be seen as noble: Think of Mr. Spock's grand speech at the end of the 1982 film *Star Trek II: The Wrath of Khan* before he... well, go watch it for yourself.[7] It's a very emotional moment and sentiment, especially coming from a person willing to make a tremendous sacrifice for the sake of others. This is a grand, heroic impulse and one to be celebrated; sacrifice for others is often considered the height of morality. But when this sacrifice is mandated or forced by an impersonal decision-making process, it is a different issue, especially when one person or group, who have done nothing to deserve the burden, are forced to sacrifice for the benefit of others who are no more deserving of their good fortune.

This problem becomes even worse when it always seems to be the same people who bear the burden time and again, in which case it becomes obvious that there *is* a reason why. This reason is often a pernicious one having nothing to do with merit or blame, but rather a lack of power and influence with those who make decisions on behalf of society. It could be a matter of certain groups having less say in government decision-making than others, whether based on corruption on the part of government agents or historical patterns of disenfranchisement and neglect. As any economist can tell you, resources are scarce and not every government initiative can be funded or every constituency served. Nonetheless, when certain initiatives or constituencies are passed over year after year, it's safe to suspect that there is a reason for this and that other parties are benefitting from it. This may seem to be the fault of a politicized or corrupted version of utilitarianism, but even pure utilitarian decision-making can result in some people receiving better treatment than others, particularly in the case of "utility monsters" who require more resources than others to experience a certain level of utility.[8]

Even when resources are distributed fairly among all constituents—and there are no utility monsters to be seen—there's no guarantee that all priorities and desires will be served, especially if there aren't enough resources to go around. Inevitably, when the scarce resources of a household, business, or government are exhausted, one program, cause, or initiative can be supported more only if another is supported less. Under utilitarianism, someone will need to decide where resources should be allocated in order to generate the highest utility overall. Utilitarian decision-making is often used to make tough choices regarding the allocation of scarce resources; this is the working definition of economics, after all, and traditional economics can be understood as utilitarian thinking put into practice.

Simply giving every person equal concern, however, does not guarantee that each person's interests and dignity will be respected. Remember what we said above: Equal treatment can also mean equal mistreatment. It is no virtue in treating everyone equally poorly or with equal disrespect; this is an ugly version of fairness indeed.

Deontology, and Kant's ethics in particular, helps correct this aspect of utilitarianism by helping to protect the rights of the individual against "ends justify the means" reasoning. Deontology in general rejects this way of thinking, maintaining that actions (the means) need to be justified in and of themselves and not simply by their consequences (the ends). For example, deontologists maintain that lying and stealing cannot be judged right or wrong by the results they lead to in any given situation, but only on the basis of the acts themselves. Generally, lying and stealing are considered to wrong, even if they lead to better outcomes overall, because they deny some essential right, duty, or principle that is considered important by deontologists. Utilitarians, however, believe lying and stealing are immoral because they usually lead to negative outcomes on the whole—but in those rare cases in which they improve outcomes, they may be allowed.

This is not to say that deontologists cannot recognize extreme situations of dire need that justify exceptions to general principle or duty. Like most utilitarians, they might excuse stealing bread to feed your starving family or taking refuge in a deserted cabin in the woods to escape the elements. Unlike utilitarians, however, deontologists would consider these to be rare exceptions to the wrongness of stealing, based on extraordinary circumstances, rather than a result of a cold comparison of the benefits and costs of stealing with no consideration for the rights, duties, or principles relevant to the situation. One variety of deontology recognizes this possibility explicitly: *Threshold deontology* says we should follow principles, duties, or rights until the cost of doing so becomes too high (or when it reaches the "threshold"), after which the decision-maker can fall back on utilitarian reasoning and act accordingly to avoid those high costs.[9] However deontology deals with extraordinary circumstances, such cases show that utilitarians and deontologists may come to the same moral judgments, even when excusing stealing or lying, but for different reasons and using different logic.

If It Pleases the Court, I'll Provide Some Examples

In general, despite their shared judgments on common and simple issues such as lying and stealing, the very different ways in which utilitarianism and deontology treat the individual imply some stark disagreements, especially when the interests of the many conflict with those of the few. The "ends justify the means" reasoning exemplified by utilitarianism often sacrifices the rights and interests of the individual when it is "necessary" to increase the well-being of the group. This is where deontology becomes important in terms of safeguarding the rights, interests, and dignity of individuals, when necessary, against utilitarianism's promotion of the interests of the whole.

Note that I said "when necessary." I want to be very careful here not to overstate my case. I am not arguing that the rights of the individual *always* take precedence over the interests of the whole. Rather, I am arguing that *sometimes* they do, that in particular circumstances, the legitimate rights of the individual should prevent actions and policies that would violate them in order to benefit a larger group in society (or a subset of it). As legal and political philosopher Ronald Dworkin put it:

> Individual rights are political trumps held by individuals. Individuals have rights when, for some reason, a collective goal is not a sufficient justification for denying them what they wish, as individuals, to have or to do, or not a sufficient justification for imposing some loss or injury upon them.[10]

As we will see later in this chapter, Dworkin's description of rights as "trumps" describes those guaranteed in the Bill of Rights to the US Constitution, such as the right to free speech, even if the content of certain speech is considered offensive or harmful to those who hear or read it, and the rights given to criminal defendants to protect them from overzealous prosecution in pursuit of justice for all. These rights protect citizens from government actions and policies in pursuit of a valid goal that may nonetheless fail to respect their basic interests.

Rights will not always trump utility, though—nor should they. Society has to find the proper balance between collective goals and respect for the individual in any given case, which can be done to some extent by legislatures but is more often, and ultimately, the responsibility of the courts, who are best positioned to make decisions regarding conflicts of principles. We will talk later about how such conflicts are resolved, but first we will discuss two recent cases in which the US Supreme Court was faced with an essential conflict between the rights of the individual and the goals of society as a whole, and chose against the interests of the individual for reasons that confirm the decline in respect for the individual we have seen throughout this book.

Eminent Domain and Kelo

Regardless of their scale or scope, most governments provide basic services such as national defense, a legal system, schools, hospitals, and infrastructure for travel (such as roads, trains, and airports). For most of these purposes, they need specific areas of land, and often this land is owned by private citizens. If the government has a good reason to need particular piece of land for a public works project, the doctrine of *eminent domain* gives them the right to purchase that land from the owner, at fair market value, even if the owner does not want to sell it.[11] While this is a violation of owners' right *not* to sell their property, the government may exercise their own right of eminent domain when there's a clear and demonstrated need for that land for the public good. In other words, eminent domain carves out a specific group of cases in which the needs of the whole are declared to take precedence over the rights of the few. Furthermore, these cases will be few and will not be arbitrary; generally, public hearings are held to demonstrate the plans and need for these projects, and property owners have the opportunity to appeal. In this way, even though the law does permit the government to violate the property rights of owners, it provides strict limits on when and how this can be done, protecting the rights of individuals as much as possible while at the same time recognizing the government's need to provide public services for all.

In recent years, however, the basis for eminent domain takings has changed in a way that compromises these protections and subjects individuals to more takings of their land with less clear justification. The traditional standard for invoking eminent domain is "public use," which justifies the forced purchase of land to build roads, schools, and hospitals, and makes clear that individuals' property can be taken only for the use (and good) of the community as a whole. But that standard has evolved into a "public good" rationale, a broader justification for authorities to forcibly purchase individuals' property in order to sell it to *other private individuals* in order to generate higher tax revenues for the government. In the typical scenario, a municipality condemns all the buildings or land in a certain area (usually a lower income neighborhood), forces the owners to sell their property to the government, and then turns around and sells it to a private developer who builds luxury homes or office parks that will bring in more property taxes for the town—the "public good" justification of the entire process.[12]

This relatively new use and justification of eminent domain represent a distinct shift in the way these government agencies treat individuals and their property rights. In the traditional understanding, government agencies could take land from private owners only in cases of clear, demonstrated, and specific public need. In the broader understanding, however, there are far fewer limits on the ability of the government to take the property of individuals, because the prospect of higher tax revenues can "justify" any forced sale of property to a developer who will build more lucrative structures on the land. The implication is that all private land is ultimately and merely a source of tax revenue for municipalities, and they're free to claim land and resell it to whomever will help them maximize those revenues, with no regard for the rights of the original landowners to refuse to sell their property (a refusal that may be based on a wide range of interests aside from pure financial gain).

In 2005, this issue reached the US Supreme Court in the case of *Kelo v. City of New London*.[13] Susette Kelo was a homeowner in New London, Connecticut, whose house was one of many in the neighborhood of Fort Trumbull that were condemned by the city to make room for a new headquarters and office park for the pharmaceutical company Pfizer. With legal assistance from the Institute for Justice, Kelo and other resistant property owners sued the town, with the case eventually reaching the Supreme Court. The Court decided for the town, deciding not to "second-guess the City's considered judgments about the efficiency of the development plan" (among other points).[14] This decision helped to solidify the modern justification for eminent domain takings, following earlier cases such as *Berman v. Parker* (1954) and *Hawaii Housing Authority v. Midkiff* (1984), both of which confirmed that, in the words of legal scholar Ilya Somin, "virtually any interest asserted by the government could qualify as a public use under the Fifth Amendment."[15]

The sum result of these decisions was to solidify the weakening of individual rights in the face of the interests of the whole, but in a particularly egregious way: sacrificing one set of private interests for another that happened to be of more use to the state. As Justice Sandra Day O'Connor wrote in her dissent, "the specter of condemnation hangs over all property.

Nothing is to prevent the State from replacing any Motel 6 with a Ritz-Carlton, any home with a shopping mall, or any farm with a factory."[16] Not only did this decision hurt the cause of property rights in general, but it is also likely to affect those least likely to assert and defend them, also pointed out by Justice O'Connor:

> Any property may now be taken for the benefit of another private party, but the fallout from this decision will not be random. The beneficiaries are likely to be those citizens with disproportionate influence and power in the political process, including large corporations and development firms. As for the victims, the government now has license to transfer property from those with fewer resources to those with more.[17]

It is quite disturbing from the point of view of the erosion of respect of the individual that in *Kelo* and the cases that preceded it, the US Supreme Court endorsed the expansion of the state's ability to violate individual property rights beyond the more reasonable and traditional public use standard to the point where a municipality's power to reassign property rights in pursuit of higher tax revenues is nearly unchecked. This is a clear sign of the shifting balance between individual and collective rights and the reliance on a brute utilitarian ethic to justify it.

The Affordable Care Act and the Individual Mandate

A more recent example of this shift can be found in the debate over the individual mandate that was one of the most significant controversies regarding the Affordable Care Act (or ACA, also popularly known as Obamacare).[18] The ACA was an attempt by the federal government to expand access to health insurance and health care at reasonable prices while also guaranteeing higher levels of coverage to the insured. To avoid the political firestorm that would be generated by even a hint of universal health care in the plan, the Obama administration and Congress attempted to achieve this goal in conjunction with existing health insurance providers rather than replacing them with a single-payer, government-run system.[19]

In any voluntary insurance program, *adverse selection* will always be a problem: The people more likely to purchase insurance will be those more likely to need it, and will likely claim more in benefits than they pay in premiums. For this reason, insurance companies also need healthy people to purchase insurance even if they don't think they will need it; on average, healthy people will pay more in premiums than they will claim in benefits, and this excess revenue for the insurance companies helps subsidize those who draw more from the system than they pay into it. There will always be some healthy individuals who are risk averse enough to buy health insurance even if they don't think they will claim more from it than they pay into it. If there aren't enough of them, however, insurance companies will be forced to raise premiums, which drives more healthy persons out of the market and guarantees only the *even* less healthy will enroll, worsening the problem and generating what is cheerily called a "death spiral."

To combat this problem, the ACA included an individual mandate which required *all* persons to have health insurance, whether through their employer and individually through one of the state insurance exchanges set up through the ACA, with penalties for noncompliance. If effective, this would help to solve the adverse selection problem by guaranteeing a large number of healthy individuals in the "risk pool" to offset the less healthy ones and keep overall premiums down (or raise revenues from those who refused to enroll, which could help offset expenditures on less healthy enrollees).

Despite this clear utilitarian rationale, the individual mandate represented an extraordinary intrusion into free choice and liberty by requiring every person, as a condition of living in the USA, to purchase a product (health insurance) from a private business. Again, this was a result of the political choice to forego a public health care system funded by general tax revenue in favor of a private system with (even) more government operation and oversight. No one is forced to buy services from their local police or fire departments, because they are funded by tax dollars; while taxation is certainly coercive, this is done to support a public good that everyone uses and no one can reasonably be excluded from. The ACA case is different in both of these ways: Rather than being forced to support the health care system through taxes, individuals are forced to purchase insurance from a private provider, not for their own good but to support the system as a whole. Furthermore, it is disputable whether health care is a public good, because individuals can be excluded (even though, by law, emergency health care services cannot be denied to patients regardless of insurance) and not all adverse health conditions are contagious.[20]

In general, the individual mandate neglected the rights of individuals to pursue their own interests—including their health interests—in the way they choose. Instead, it used them as a means to support a collective health care system that they would not otherwise have participated in (as evidenced by the coercive enforcement mechanism built into the system).

Some legal scholars, most notably Randy Barnett, argued that this was a wrongful intrusion on liberty rights (that, ironically, could have avoided if the government had gone full in on a public health care system).[21] Because the administration and Congress tried to mimic the outcomes of the public system on the foundation of the existing private system, they failed to respect the nature of either, falling short of the desired effects of a public system while imposing excessive controls on the private system—and the individuals that participate in it (voluntarily or not).

The strength of Barnett's criticism was highlighted by the government's main argument in support of the individual mandate: that the Commerce Clause, a constitutional provision that grants the federal government the right "to regulate commerce... among the several States," extended to individual's purchase *and refusal to purchase* private health insurance.[22] Much to the delight of this philosopher, much of this debate became downright metaphysical, hinging on whether refusing to buy something was an "act" that could be regulated.[23] Regardless of the merits of the rest of the debate over the ACA (or universal health care in general), the extension of the Commerce Clause to cover individual choices whether or not to purchase a good, in the absence of any involvement with interstate commerce, is a dangerous precedent with enormous potential impact on the interests and choices of individuals.

Precisely this point was highlighted when the dispute over the individual mandate (and other aspects of the ACA) reached the Supreme Court in the case of *National Federation of Independent Businesses (NFIB) vs. Sebelius* in 2011.[24] The majority decision issued the following year, written by Chief Justice John Roberts, confirmed Barnett's argument regarding the unconstitutionality of the individual mandate. In it, Chief Justice Roberts referred to the nature of refusal to buy insurance when he wrote that "allowing Congress to justify federal regulation by pointing to the effect of inaction on commerce would bring countless decisions an individual could potentially make within the scope of federal regulation, and—under the Government's theory—empower Congress to make those decisions for him."[25] "Congress already enjoys vast power to regulate much of what we do," he continued. "Accepting the Government's theory would give Congress the same license to regulate what we do not do."[26] In his conclusion, Chief Justice Roberts asserted that "the individual mandate cannot be upheld as an exercise of Congress's power under the Commerce Clause. That Clause authorizes Congress to regulate interstate commerce, *not to order individuals to engage in it.*"[27]

The Court did, however, reinterpret the mandate as a tax rather than a penalty in order to preserve its spirit, leaving the ACA mostly unaffected by the decision that nonetheless refuted the central argument in its favor.[28] Legal technicalities aside—apologies to my law professor friends—this result, despite the language of the Chief Justice to the contrary, represents yet another shift in the balance between the individual and society. The preservation of the individual mandate moves this balance strongly to the side of the latter, granting the state immeasurable discretion to interfere with the choices of individuals—as illustrated by the suggestion, widely made by critics at the time but never successfully refuted by supporters of the ACA, that broccoli consumption could be mandated to lower society's health care costs.[29]

Outside the issue of the individual mandate, the concept of universal health care also carries its own negative implications regarding the interests and rights of the individual, even for those who accept that publically provided health care is a positive thing. The most significant concern follows from the utilitarian reasoning at its heart, specifically in the presumption of public funding for health care. When individuals are responsible for their own health care costs, even in conjunction with their insurance companies, the ultimate decision whether they feel a health care intervention is justified or not is theirs. As a result, individuals, along with their family, doctors, and insurance provider, can decide whether they want to devote their resources to more or less expensive treatments in the context of their overall interests, both financial and otherwise.

If the state takes responsibility for all health care costs of its citizens and residents, however, those decisions are removed from the domain of individuals and those close to them and relegated instead to distant bureaucrats. These bureaucrats will behave much like insurance companies do now, trying to minimize costs while providing the mandated level of care—which, like insurance companies currently, they will have the power to influence. Decisions whether to devote more resources to care are taken out of the hands of individuals, their family, and their doctors, and vested in bureaucrats who know nothing of the personal circumstances or interests of patients but know everything about the costs of care, which will be their primary focus as they try to manage the financial outlays of a massive health care system while staying within legal limits regarding minimal required care.

Furthermore, unlike insurance companies, the government also has the power to mandate certain behaviors—the least of which may be broccoli consumption—in the interests of lowering public health care costs.

Although the health care system in the USA is nowhere near as universalized as those in Canada, the UK, or Europe, we should expect to see more regulation of health behaviors as the government assumes more responsibility for health care costs; already, we can see taxes and nudges targeting sugary drinks, stricter regulation of smoking, and other behavioral interventions, all motivated, in part, by lowering the public health expenditures from Medicare and Medicaid, a trend that will only increase in speed and scale as the government assumes a greater share of health care costs on behalf of its citizens.[30]

All Is Not Lost…

While cases such as these two provide examples of decisions that set aside the respect and concern for the individual in favor of collective interests, there are other important Supreme Court decisions that protect individual interests as well. For example, the 2008 decision in *District of Columba v. Heller* confirmed the reading of the Second Amendment that protects the right of the individual to bear arms (rather than a more restrictive view that applies to government entities such as police and militia), even if the protection of this right may be associated with a greater incidence of gun violence.[31] The 2010 decision in *Citizens United v. Federal Election Commission* endorsed the freedom of organizations such as corporations and labor unions to donate to political campaigns on behalf of their owners or members, even though some see a corruptive effect on the electoral and political process from such contributions.[32] Both decisions affirmed rights of the individual despite otherwise valid concerns in the collective interest and counterbalance, to some extent, the deterioration of individual rights seen in *Kelo* and *NFIB* (although the outsized reactions from some quarters to *Heller* and *Citizens United* might diminish some of the enthusiasm on that front).[33] Later in this chapter, we'll look at another even more recent case that affirmed important rights of individuals, although the way it was done did not please even those who agreed with the outcome, which is suggestive in its own right of the decline in respect for the individual.

RIGHTS ARE IMPORTANT BUT NOT ABSOLUTE

As we saw in the cases mentioned above, regardless of how they were decided, individual and collective interests often conflict, and when they do, they must be balanced. This is not a flaw but a feature of liberal democracies that recognize the importance of both, with the "proper" balance shifting over time as both individuals and societies develop and their respective priorities change. In the eminent domain and health care examples in particular, however, we can see the weight put on the interests and dignity of the individual in those and other cases declining in favor of an increasing concern with the aggregate or whole, in part due to the various influences we surveyed earlier in this book.

The roots of this balance can be found in the central political and legal documents in most liberal democracies. In the USA, they are found primarily in the Bill in Rights, the first ten amendments to the Constitution. Many of the familiar guarantees of individual rights found there, such as freedom of speech, association, religion, and the press, can be interpreted as Dworkin's "trumps," which restrain the government from neglecting the essential rights of individuals when conducting policy in the interests of the country as a whole. As the First Amendment reads, the state shall pass no law "abridging the freedom of speech, or of the press, of the right of the people to peaceably assemble," even when—or *especially* when—such a law might very well increase overall well-being. Regardless of their impact or consequences, these rights, and the choices, interests, and dignity they protect, are considered to be essential to the full lives of individual in a liberal society.

Nonetheless, there are exceptions to these guarantees, and this epitomizes the sense of balance needed while leaving room for individual and collective interests to be balanced in unique ways in specific cases. For example, freedom of speech is one of the most cherished rights of the individual in the USA and other liberal societies. Traditionally, the right of individuals to express their thoughts and feelings in whatever forum they have access to is sacrosanct, extending even to the most hateful and vile speech. Of course, this right does not come with the right to use anyone else's forum; no newspaper, website, or organization has to host speech they don't like (which in turn is an expression of their own free speech rights). Nor does this right absolve anyone of the consequences of expressing unpopular opinions, including speech in disagreement, ridicule, and shaming—but not violence, against which the law protects the speaker as it does in the context of any other lawful behavior.

This right is held in such high esteem that even speech that can reasonably be argued to lower overall welfare is protected. The paradigmatic example is the racist spewing hate on the street corner or marching with fellow-minded individuals in a parade. This kind of expression is very likely to cause significant emotional distress to targeted individuals and communities as well as those who support them in solidarity with the cause of human equality and dignity. Despite the negative effect overall—most probably in excess of whatever personal satisfaction the racist gets from self-expression—the right of the individual to speak his or her mind is protected, as reflected in the famous quote, often attributed to either Voltaire or the historian Evelyn Beatrice Hall, "I disapprove of what you say, but I will defend to the death your right to say it."[34]

This is not to say, however, that there are no cases in which free speech may be limited in the interests of the community—just that these limitations are usually not based on the political or ideological content of the speech, implying that offense and even significant distress are not sufficient to counterbalance the right to speak. The most well-known exception to the right of free speech is probably "clear and present danger," as expressed by Supreme Court Justice Oliver Wendell Holmes in the 1919 case *Schenck v. United States*.[35] For example, he wrote that "the most stringent protection of free speech would not protect a man falsely shouting fire in a theater and causing a panic," because that would likely cause panic and potentially injury, with little countervailing value in terms of promoting free expression and exchange of ideas.[36] For similar reasons, free speech is not protected if it is clearly meant to incite violence or "imminent lawless action," as written in the 1969 decision *Brandenburg v. Ohio*.[37] These exceptions show that even the right to free speech is not absolute and can be set aside when collective interests clearly outweigh even the tremendous importance assigned to those of the individual.

In recent years, however, this right to free speech has been questioned beyond these traditional understandings, and limitations on that right have been proposed on grounds of its substance, justified by the harm or disrespect inflicted by particularly hurtful forms of "hate speech" understood to target minority populations. This became a widely publicized matter during the campaign leading to the 2016 presidential election, when long-bubbling tensions along lines of class, race, gender, and religion came to the surface, and was most visibly symbolized in controversial speakers being disinvited from campuses around the country. While these acts didn't affect these speakers' freedom of speech in general—they had other opportunities to express themselves—and reflected the rights of the universities to refuse a forum to certain speech, the fact that these rejections came from universities which, traditionally, have been the home of the free expression, debate, and exchange of ideas, is troubling to many.[38]

This trend shifts the balance farther away from the speech rights of the individual, going beyond the limitations established in *Schenck* and *Brandenberg* by either broadening the exceptions to free speech to include offense, or incorporating the harm from offensive speech into the definition of violence.[39] This is troubling to those who support minimal limits of speech, regard more speech as always preferred to less, and maintain that the best answer to harmful speech is more speech in disagreement with it. As John Stuart Mill wrote in the second chapter to *On Liberty*, titled "Of the Liberty of Thought and Discussion,"

> the peculiar evil of silencing the expression of an opinion is, that it is robbing the human race; posterity as well as the existing generation; those who dissent from the opinion, still more than those who hold it. If the opinion is right, they are deprived of the opportunity of exchanging error for truth: if wrong, they lose, what is almost as great a benefit, the clearer perception and livelier impression of truth, produced by its collision with error.[40]

This argument is a pragmatic one focused on the value of speech more than the right of individuals to express themselves, which shows that a maximal right to free speech can be defended on a utilitarian basis as well as on a deontological one focused on rights. Also, Mill's statement highlights the wisdom of a certain degree of *epistemic humility*, the recognition that we are not always right and someone else may know better in some cases, a possibility better realized by more speech rather than less.

But is there a point at which harmful speech becomes too harmful, where speech runs the risk of being wrong not on the basis of evidence or argument but in terms of morality? For example, advocates for greater limits on free speech argue that when speech denies certain groups of people full personhood or legitimacy as participants, allowing that speech actually limits open debate and exchange of ideas by implicitly excluding some people from it. As literature professor and vice provost at New York University Urlich Baer argued, "Some topics, such as claims that some human beings are by definition inferior to others, or illegal or unworthy of legal standing, are not open to debate because such people cannot debate them on the same terms."[41] The people targeted by such speech are free to assert their existence and legitimacy as equal participants, of course, but this can reasonably be considered an unfair burden, especially to those who already feel marginalized in society. It is not inconsistent to maintain that the best answer to a bad idea is a better argument and also that it should not always be the responsibility of the persons most affected by those bad ideas to fight back against them. A better answer may be for others, whether individuals or institutions, to offer more support to marginalized persons in combatting the harmful speech rather than suppressing it altogether. Nonetheless, the concern is reasonable, even if the impulse to prohibit potentially harmful speech that is becoming standard is likely to do more harm than good in the long run.[42]

We must also acknowledge that the judgments of whether particular speech has a dehumanizing impact are also subject to question. A Nazi is a Nazi, obviously, but most disinvited speakers are not Nazis, and it's unclear where the line should be drawn—or who should draw it. Once you open the door to limiting speech on grounds of substance, you have to ask: Who is going to decide what substance is disqualified, and will these persons have the epistemic humility to recognize that even a controversial speaker may have something to offer? Again, Mill wrote wisely on this:

> Strange that they should imagine that they are not assuming infallibility, when they acknowledge that there should be free discussion on all subjects which can possibly be *doubtful*, but think that some particular principle or doctrine should be forbidden to be questioned because it is *so certain*, that is, because *they are certain* that it is certain. To call any proposition certain, while there is any one who would deny its certainty if permitted, but who is not permitted, is to assume that we ourselves, and those who agree with us, are the judges of certainty, and judges without hearing the other side.[43]

This is perhaps the most disturbing aspect of the suppression of the free expression and exchange of ideas on college campuses: the presumption of college students to know, with absolute certainty, that certain propositions are wrong and should not be presented and discussed. If a position is obviously incorrect, students who know this should have no problem arguing against it—and many do, as can be seen in videos shot when controversial speakers are allowed to present their ideas and face criticism from those in attendance.

Another question to ask is: Will the person or persons given authority to block speech always be on *your* side? Even if you are legitimately and significantly offended or hurt by the expression of certain ideas, granting a select few the power to restrict it may be used later to restrict speech you support. Limitations on the speech rights of the individual are often promoted as benefiting individuals, especially those who feel dehumanized by particularly harmful speech, based on inequities in power and who is "served" most by free speech. Throughout history, however, free speech has been one of the most powerful tools to improve the well-being of the marginalized and disenfranchised against those who would oppress them; the greatest tragedy would be if limitations on speech meant to benefit just these people ended up harming their interests in the long run. As journalist Conor Friedersdorf argued in response to Baer, how are heinous, dehumanizing opinions and positions supposed to be refuted "if the next generation of educational elites is prevented from debating or even mentioning the matter in the one setting where they are training to reason well?"[44] To suppress such ideas or remove them from public debate risks emboldening those who hold them, who then become "martyrs" to their "cause," helping to spread those ideas in the minds of those who find the repression of their speech to be a form of confirmation of their validity.

In a broader sense, this debate about free speech—which, ironically, relies itself on the freedom of speech—can be seen as a specific instance of the struggle of liberal society to tolerance intolerance. How far should such a society, or groups within it, accommodate the expression of ideas that question the root of tolerance itself? At some point, is the liberal society entitled to say "enough"? These are difficult questions and ones that unfortunately, we will be dealing with more and more in the years to come, but the answer should always be sought on the side of respecting the dignity of the individual, including his or her right to thought and expression, as much as possible.

Beware the Tyranny of the Majority

A more general danger to respect for the individual can be put in terms of what John Stuart Mill called a "tyranny of the majority."[45] While he was very aware of the danger of a tyrannical government acting in the interests of the ruling class, Mill also wanted to highlight the threat of overreach even from the most democratic of governments, with elected representatives sincerely acting in the interests of their constituents, but not necessary respecting the rights of all of them. This concept is often misinterpreted as a critique of majority rule in general, but Mill meant to criticize specific cases in which the majority votes to pursue a policy at the expense of the essential rights of the minority.

In the USA, the individual rights guaranteed in the Constitution and defended by the courts can be understood as helping to prevent a tyranny of the majority. It is for this reason that an overwhelmingly Christian community cannot vote to block the construction of a mosque; a majority white community cannot pass laws that prevent blacks from participating in civic affairs; and a liberal tolerant community cannot prevent a white supremacist group from gathering, even to spread their messages of hate (although this is changing, as we saw). Even before Mill, this danger was on the mind of those who crafted the Bill of Rights; as we saw earlier, the language "Congress shall pass no law" prevents the state for pursuing the legitimate interests of the majority if pursuing those interests means denying others their essential rights.

Even though no discrimination or bias need be present to create a tyranny of the majority—wrongful eminent domain takings, for instance, could be described as a tyranny of the majority, with the elected representatives in a town denying the property rights of the few—the clearest examples come from the denial of civil rights to minority groups based solely on the "preferences" of the majority, with no valid recognized interest in the matter, but rather trying to preserve the status quo. The struggles for marriage rights for interracial and same-sex couples are one such example: The opinions of the majority of voters, as expressed through their elected representatives, stood in the way of recognizing these marriages which advocates believed should be allowed based on the principle if not settled law. It ultimately fell to the Supreme Court in both cases to recognize and protect the rights of individuals in the minority to marry the persons of their choice.[46]

Furthermore, these decisions had the positive effect of denying any relevance to the majority voters' preferences regarding other people's marriages, even when the majority supported the rights of the minority. Particularly in the case of same-sex marriage, many states had voted to allow it even before the Supreme Court decision, and many people argued that the matter should be left to the voters rather than be imposed by the courts. If marriage equality is a matter of right, however, it should not be subject to popular vote even if the majority was likely to approve it. Rights are not a matter for popular vote; even when the majority votes in favor of the minority, it is still a tyranny of the majority to the extent that they have a say on essential rights at all. It is important that the right of adults to marry the person of their choice, regardless of gender or race, was recognized as an essential right by the Court to be truly valid *as a right* rather than merely a privilege "granted" by a benevolent majority.

Mind you, this is not to say that the Supreme Court is perfect in their role as the protector of individual rights against the will of the majority. Aside from the recent cases we discussed earlier, they have made profoundly horrible decisions in the past, such as *Plessy v. Ferguson*, which endorsed racial segregation, and *Korematsu v. United States*, which approved the internment of Japanese Americans during World War II.[47] Ideally, however, as we will see in the next section, the courts play an integral role in protecting the rights of the individual against government action based on the preferences of the electorate as a whole, regardless of the morality of those preferences.

We can now see that the status and importance of the individual are under threat from two directions identified above. From one side, an increasing concern for the welfare of the community as a whole, and the accompanying dismissal of the rights of the individual, is enabling a tyranny of the majority in which those rights are more often being lessened. But also, the spread of explicitly intolerant movements tests the limits of even the most liberal, tolerant society to maintain even a formal respect of the rights of those who would deny such rights to others. In this way, the rights of the individual are being eroded from within liberal society and from without, making a restoration of respect and consideration for the individual more imperative than ever.

Finding a Balance Among Conflicting Principles

Throughout this chapter, we've been discussing the need to balance the legitimate interests of the individual with those of society as a whole. The importance of balancing conflicting principles was emphasized by Ronald Dworkin, whom we met earlier in the context of the idea that individual rights must sometimes trump collective welfare. His work gives us a different way to think about the cases we discussed above, as well as the general problems we face to balancing the needs of the individual and society.

Dworkin split the responsibilities of government into two types: policies and principles.[48] Policies are the goals that reflect the interests and preferences of the citizens, such as national defense, education, health care, and infrastructure. These are the initiatives that voters elect representatives to further; these representatives meet in legislative bodies where they discuss the various goals demanded by their respective constituencies, and those goals with the support of the majority of voters (and their representatives) are pursued. (Ideally, of course—this isn't Schoolhouse Rock, after all.) As the demography and political preferences of the electorate shift, their priorities shift, as we see when the presidency or the majorities in Congress change parties.

Principles, however, are very different; they represent timeless ideals that are embedded into the core of a society's legal–political system and are therefore less subject to change with the political winds. The guarantees of individual freedoms guaranteed in the Bill of Rights, such as the rights to free speech, religion, and peaceful assembly, can be understood as formalized versions of basic principles at the heart of the country. But these principles need not be written into official law: For example, the statements in the Declaration of Independence, recognizing that individuals have "certain inalienable rights" including "life, liberty, and the pursuit of happiness," can also be considered essential principles of American society and government. In general, principles are the core ideas of a society or country which guide—or constrain—the government's action in the interest of policy. Most importantly for our purposes, some principles help protect individuals from a tyranny of the majority in making sure that even laws and policies enacted through a legitimate legislative process cannot be pursued if they violate essential rights of individuals.

Of course, these rights, both in their definition and in their scope, are inherently vague and as such are subject to debate and interpretation. As we know from earlier in this chapter, even the right to free speech, traditionally valued above most other rights of the individual, is not absolute, even in its broadest sense. The simple directive that "Congress shall make no law… abridging the freedom of speech" is anything but precise or definite, as we see in various Supreme Court decisions over the years. How judges can and should interpret constitutional language in order to issue decisions in cases that involve a conflict of principles is at the heart of the field of legal philosophy called *jurisprudence*. Terms from this field such as "originalism" and "the Living Constitution" become part of the national discussion each time a president's nominee for the Supreme Court is questioned by the Senate Judiciary Committee, and the contentious debate over them in the legal academy is but one indication of how fraught—and fascinating—constitutional interpretation is.[49]

In his own work, Dworkin described how principles should be balanced against each other according to their weight in particular circumstances, especially when confronted by the courts in "hard cases." The most controversial topics of argument, whether among a nation's citizens and within its government, are inevitably those that involve a conflict of basic principles, and this applies most obviously to cases that climb through the court system to its highest level, which in the USA is the Supreme Court. While our elected representatives in the White House and Congress debate which policies the government will pursue and promote, the Supreme Court serves to protect, enforce, and refine our understanding of the essential principles within which the government makes policy. Traditionally, the Supreme Court doesn't make decisions on policy itself unless a particular policy is found to infringe on individual rights, such as when it decides on school segregation (*Brown v. Board of Education*), detention during wartime (*Boumediene v. Bush*), or, as we discussed above, the rights of interracial and same-sex couples to marry (*Loving* and *Obergefell*).[50] All of these cases dealt with the essential rights of individuals, reflecting core principles of the country as maintained and interpreted by the Supreme Court justices at the time, that were being violated by the government policy in question. As Dworkin wrote, judges do not create rights when they make groundbreaking decisions, but simply assert and formalize rights that always existed based on essential principles of the legal system. In other words, individuals always *deserved* these rights, but they weren't recognized officially by law until the Supreme Court wrote them into decisions in hard cases.

When the Supreme Court decides between individual rights and social interests, they're striking a balance based on how much weight the individual justices feel each concern deserves in that particular context. Of course, that balance will not always be found on the side of the individual, and all the cases we have criticized in this chapter can be interpreted in terms of this judicial balancing. Obviously, the decisions in *Plessy* and *Korematsu* failed to give even the minimal respect and consideration owned to the affected individuals when considering the impact on them of segregation and internment (respectively). In *Kelo*, the Supreme Court dismissed the property rights of individuals in favor of a city whose main interest was increasing property tax revenues, and in *NFIB*, the court acknowledged and then set aside concerns over forcing individuals to buy health insurance in order to protect the system established by the Affordable Care Act (ultimately reading the statutory terms differently to circumvent the constitutional objections they earlier agreed were valid). We can acknowledge the Court's difficult job in balancing conflicting principles and give them the benefit of the doubt that they gave fair consideration to all principles relevant to the case and still criticize their decision when it fails to give sufficient respect to the individual in the face of social policymaking.

While recent cases such as *Kelo* and *NFIB* reflect poorly on the cause of respect for the individual, we must acknowledge positive signs, such as *Heller*, *Citizens United*, and particularly *Obergefell*, in which the right of same-sex couples to marry was recognized. Cases like *Obergefell*—and *Loving*, *Brown*, and *Plessy* before it—are different from most of the others we have discussed. In cases such as *Kelo* and *NFIB*, both sides had mutually acknowledged valid interests, one protecting the individual and the other furthering a legitimate goal of the electorate expressed through their legislators. Each side could, in theory, acknowledge the validity of the other side's positions—even in emotional debates over issues such as abortion, euthanasia, and the death penalty—although each side obviously feels their argument is stronger and their claim more valid. In cases like *Obergefell* and the rest, however, there is no room for agreement. Each side views the interests of the other side as illegitimate, the two sides are pushing in opposite directions, and as a result, no common ground can be found. Those favoring a more traditional view of marriage found their justification in tradition, religion, or natural law, and dismissed the desire of same-sex couples to marry on those grounds (as many regarded interracial marriage a half-century earlier). On the other side, same-sex and interracial couples (and their allies) asserted their own rights as human beings to marry the person of their choice and declared the interests of their opponents invalid on the basis of outdated, racist, or homophobic attitudes.[51]

This additional element in these cases makes a balanced consideration of them nearly impossible, because it is very difficult to give comparable moral weight to two perspectives that contradict each other. We can't endorse the moral and legal right of all persons to marry whomever they want while also granting others the right to deny it. However, a solid basis of respect for individuals and their interests would favor the rights of interracial and same-sex couples who want to marry, regardless of the impressions and feelings of anyone else. Even if we were to give defenders of traditional marriage the benefit of the doubt and assume their beliefs were not based on animus toward homosexuals (or blacks, in the case of interracial marriage), there is no reason why their preferences over the matter should have any impact of the rights of other people to marry. As we said above, even if the majority decided to "grant" interracial and same-sex couples this right, it is not their right to grant, but rather belongs to each individual already, whether or not it is formally recognized by law. In its *Obergefell* decision, the Supreme Court recognized this right and wrote it into law in a striking endorsement for the rights of the individual (although not in denial of any valid collective interests).

The Individual and the Politics of Left Versus Right

How does the issue of the rights of the individual versus the concerns of the whole map onto our usual political distinction between the left and the right? A simplistic view of American politics would say that the right favors the individual while the left favors society, but that would confuse and conflate many different issues. No side, party, or ideology has a monopoly on concern for the rights of the individual or the rejection of government initiatives that violate those rights. As usual, the left–right distinction, based on the French National Assembly *après la révolution*, fails to capture the complexity of real-world politics. (We'll keep the Statue of Liberty, *mes amies*, but you can have the left–right thing back.)

Traditionally, each side of the political spectrum defends particular individual rights and neglects others. The right typically emphasizes individual rights in the realm of economics and the market—such as in the case of the individual mandate in the ACA—while the left prefers to focus on collective goals of markets (and limitations thereof). Likewise, those on the left are more concerned with state interference with individual rights in the areas on marriage, sex, and reproduction, while those on the right are usually content to let traditional understandings and practices regarding these activities remain the subject of government policy. Anyone who has observed the activism in support of the rights of women to control their bodies or homosexuals to marry cannot doubt the passion among the left for certain rights of the individual—but not rights in the marketplace, which are traditionally the domain of those on the right.

Libertarians see no distinction between "economic" and "personal" rights, viewing them all as essential rights of individuals to pursue their interests, which must be protected against the policy actions of the state.[52] As such, they were just as active in arguments supporting the legalization of same-sex marriage as they were in the arguments against the ACA individual mandate and the abuse of eminent domain. Libertarians argue that there is no distinction between economic and noneconomic rights because both protect choices that individuals make in their interests. We all need the freedom to use our personal resources in the way we choose to order to pursue our interests and express our individual identities—which is not to say we have *positive rights* or claims to resources, which libertarians would maintain infringe on the liberties of others, but we do have *negative rights* to be free from illegitimate interference with how we use those resources, which should be protected as strongly as our rights regarding our thoughts, speech, and bodies.[53] Unfortunately, however, the survival of this artificial distinction is reflected in recent Supreme Court decisions that affirm the noneconomic rights of individuals (such as *Obergefell*) but not their economic ones (*Kelo*, *NFIB*). If this is indicative of a pattern, it's an encouraging one with respect to the "personal" rights of individuals but not their "economic" ones.

As with individuals, governments are free to pursue whatever social goals they choose—ideally, reflecting the will of the people—but not to the exclusion or violation of the essential rights of individuals. This mirrors, in a way, the point made earlier about the dual nature of the individuals, who can pursue their own interests as autonomous, distinct persons but always within the bounds of respect for the rights of other individuals. Individuals must balance all of their own preferences and goals with their duties toward others, both negative ones that respect the autonomy and dignity of others and positive ones that reflect concern and beneficence.[54] The rights of individuals and the principles they are based on represent constraints on the actions we can take, even in the interests of others—and the same holds for government as well. Modern liberal systems of governments were established to protect the rights of individuals while allowing government latitude to take policy action within those bounds. We must resist the temptation to loosen those constraints, especially in light of the scientific and humanistic trends identified in the first chapters of this book that would seem to dim the luster of the individual's cognitive and moral capacities and open the door for more unrestrained utilitarian thinking that relies on our similarities without respecting our differences (which is especially relevant in this age of increasing attention and respect paid to diversity and multiculturalism).

And Where Does Business Fit in?

In the last two chapters, we've talked about individuals and governments in terms of their attitudes and obligations toward persons, but we left one important group out: business. (We'll return to the government in the next section.) At the risk of understatement, in market-oriented economies businesses are very influential decision-makers, affecting the lives of individuals and the success of government policies. But they do so in a unique way, at least as they're normally understood: Businesses have a dual nature in that they act as individual decision-makers in their own interests, usually profit, while they're also understood to have a public role to some extent that obligates them to certain pro-social activity, such as charitable and principled behavior above and beyond the minimal requirements of ethics and law. In this sense, a business is self-oriented in its decision-making, while also understood to have a public role without necessarily clear public responsibilities.

The typical view of business is that of the single-minded (if not rapacious) profit-maximizing entity that makes every decision, from pricing and product mix to working conditions and public relations, with its eye solely on the bottom line. While this may be less inappropriate than the picture of the individual as purely self-interested, it still misses much of the ethical nuance involved in business. While we speak of business as if it were a single entity—which does apply to the self-employed, of course—most businesses are made up of a collection of individuals, each of whom makes his or her decisions according to that person's role and responsibility (as well as interests). As a result of individuals' cooperation within the structure of the business, these collective decisions result in the actions the business takes in the world outside its walls with respect to its customers, business partners, government, and the broader public.

A business's relationships with the people who make it up and with parties outside its walls (physical or metaphorical) highlight the two ways in which a business may have responsibilities that transcend its own profit, responsibilities that are often taken for granted when we speak of businesses as pure, single-minded profit maximizers. Many of these responsibilities are enforced by law, others by norms or common practices, and yet others by market competition, but some are the more autonomous choices of those who run a business and determine its culture related to ethical behavior.

Regarding the people who make it up, a company must, at minimum, treat them with the respect owed all persons, as any individual or government must do, including avoiding coercion or deceit in how they are treated within the business. Of course, businesses must go beyond that in their terms of employment, including contracted provisions such as wage, salary, and benefits, and a certain role in the operation of the business and within its hierarchy. There is considerable variety in the compensation packages and corporate structures at companies, who are free to experiment with both in an effort to retain the best employees and create value within the company. Some are better at this than others: For example, Google and Wegman's are well known for their pro-employee culture in which cooperation, consideration, and respect are emphasized.[55] As we said, these aspects of a work culture may be a matter of market competition to attract and retain the best employees, but to some extent, they may also be an expression of the business leaders' attitude toward their employees, above and beyond what is necessary by law, norms, or competition.

While business's responsibility toward its employees is often taken for granted, its behavior toward parties in the outside world, especially their customers and the public as a whole, is more widely emphasized, especially in the enormous literature on business ethics. Narrowly considered, a business has the same duties to avoid coercion and deceit to its customers and business partners that any individual has, and these limits are often required by law. Beyond that, a business may assume no further social responsibilities beside producing and selling a product or service that its customers are willing to purchase; in fact, economist Milton Friedman famously argued that this should be understood, by society and business managers alike, to be a private company's *only* responsibility (within the bounds of law, ethics, and market norms).[56]

Nonetheless, businesses (or the decision-makers within them) are free to embrace broader social responsibilities such as taking measures to protect the environment or donating to charitable causes. Again, such actions may reflect sincere concern on the part of the business ownership or it may be a calculated public relations ploy (sometimes called "greenwashing" in the case of environmental action or "pinkwashing" in the case of support of LGBTQ issues), which resembles the complex and multifaceted interests of the individual and the many explanations one can imagine for any particular behavior. Although businesses have a clearer singular interest than individuals have—presumptively speaking, profit—their pursuit of that interest, specifically in light of the other goals and constraints they face, makes them seem more like the individuals we have been looking at throughout this book (with all their attendant faults and shortcomings).

Of particular interest in this context is the argument from some quarters that, contrary to Friedman, business not only can but *should* assume some degree of social responsibility based on their position in society.[57] In this view, all businesses are public concerns, operating at the pleasure of the government and as such have responsibilities toward the public deriving from that government-endowed status. This can be contrasted with the view that businesses are initiatives of individuals, acting alone or together, to use their resources to earn a profit by selling a product or service to consumers, much in the same way that a worker sells his labor to earn wages and a saver lends her capital to earn interest from those who can put it to better use. To argue that a business has general responsibilities to the public above and beyond honest and noncoercive dealings with their customers involves additional assumptions about the nature of a business that are not easily derived from this simple understanding.

There is some rationale for the public nature of corporations, which are not "natural" forms of business. While any number of investors can jointly combine to form or purchase a business, each one owning a certain number of shares in that business, it takes a positive act of government to grant those owners limited liability, which many would say contributed to the rise of the modern corporation.[58] Because corporations owe their existence to this act of government, acting on behalf of the public, it would not be unreasonable to suggest that corporations owe a greater responsibility to the public in exchange. To some extent, they do have more legal responsibilities: For example, publically traded corporations have obligations to provide open access to financial data. But there is no clear obligation to support more general social causes or provide a higher-than-normal level of pay of working conditions for its employees in exchange for the grant of limited liability, from which the rest of society can be argued to benefit as well.[59]

Even if we were to accept some degree of social responsibility on the part of corporations, there would be no such obligation on the part of other forms of business, such as sole proprietorships or small partnerships (even if classified, technically, as corporations for tax purposes). These businesses don't enjoy limited liability, and in this sense, they are no different from laborers or savers that also use their resources for personal gain. Of course, small businesses are rarely expected to contribute to social causes such as environmental or social justice in the same way or at the same scale that corporations are (other than supporting community activities such as local softball teams and bowling leagues).

One area in which the social responsibility of small businesses has been invoked recently involves the freedom to refuse service to certain customers (often same-sex couples) on religious grounds. Most of us will be familiar with headline-making cases in recent years dealing with wedding bakers and photographers refusing on religious grounds to provide services for same-sex weddings, or small businesses contesting for similar reasons the ACA requirement that they provide contraception to employees through their health plans (with one such case, *Burwell v. Hobby Lobby*, making it to the Supreme Court).[60] What all these cases have in common is a conflict between the individual right to follow one's religious convictions and the societal interest in promoting tolerance of private behavior related to marriage and sex—or, if we dig deeper, a conflict between two mutually exclusive acts of individual expression, one related to religion and the other related to sexual identity and behavior.

There is a lot to disentangle here, in particular with respect to how we treat religious restrictions when they conflict with public policy, and it is not my goal here to do the disentangling or to pronounce for one side or the other.[61] The aspect of these cases of interest here is the presumption that businesses must set aside the religious convictions of their owners because of a public purpose or role. While engaged couples are free to decide, based on religious preferences, not to hire photographers or bakers who openly identify as homosexual, photographers or bakers are not granted the same latitude because the public nature of their business is presumed to preclude them from denying service to customers on grounds of their sexual orientation. You don't have to endorse these attitudes or choices to acknowledge that in such cases, religious liberties are constrained more for business owners than for private individuals. This asymmetry between business and customer implies a greater social obligation or responsibility on the part of businesses because they are understood to have some sort of public role, as opposed to an understanding of business as an expression of individual initiative in which the obligations of both sides of the transaction are equivalent (for better or for worse).

This presumed public role also explains many of the regulations on businesses designed to steer their behavior in the interests of the whole, to the exclusion of their rights as individuals engaging in commerce. This is not to question regulations that guarantee the safety of workers or consumers, or similar basic legal protections, but rather those that constrain the decisions businesses make in the marketplace in the interest of certain market outcomes such as lower prices or higher output, both of which contribute to what economists called "consumer surplus," the utility that consumers enjoy above and beyond the price they pay for goods and services. Examples of such regulations include limits of the prices businesses may legally set for their products (price floors and ceilings), the wages they may pay their workers (such as minimum wage laws), and their freedom to communicate, cooperate, or combine with other businesses (as enforced through antitrust law).

Although there are clear and valid rationales for each of these constraints on business conduct, most of them have to do with guaranteeing a certain level of well-being for consumers or workers above and beyond what they would presumably be able to expect in the unconstrained marketplace. However, this comes at the expense of the interests and rights of individuals in their role as business owners, with little explicit justification besides a general impression among the public and government that businesses "owe" the public something more than the honest dealings businesses expect from their partners in trade.[62] So pernicious is this impression that the Supreme Court case that most famously contradicted it, *Lochner v. New York*, is now held by most legal commentators to be almost as misguided as *Plessy* and *Koramatsu*, even though *Lochner* can be interpreted as protecting the rights of individuals against the interests of the whole.[63]

This doesn't imply that businesses should be encouraged to be rapacious profit maximizers and care nothing for the interests of others. If businesses are to be treated not as extensions of the government and sources of employment and tax revenue but individuals acting together in their own right, their choices made in their own interests need to be respected just as we should respect those of individuals acting in any capacity. The state-granted benefits of limited liability to corporations aside, it is difficult to see why individuals acting as producers and sellers owe any more to society that any other individual does or why they should not enjoy the same rights. Another widely reviled Supreme Court decision we discussed earlier, *Citizens United*, endorses this interpretation of businesses as extensions of individuals. Despite the popular misunderstanding of the opinion that holds it to have declared corporations and unions to have personhood, *Citizens United* merely confirmed that groups of individuals such as corporations and unions act as conduits through which the individuals that make them up can exercise their rights—in this case, their rights of free speech. As Justice Antonin Scalia wrote in his concurring opinion, "All the provisions of the Bill of Rights set forth the rights of individual men and women. ... But the individual person's right to speak includes the right to speak in association with other individual persons."[64] In other words, individuals do not lose their essential rights when they form groups and speak through those groups, nor should they be burdened with additional legal or social obligations as because they choose to engage in commerce with other individuals.[65]

It may not be intuitive to think of businesses, especially large corporations, as collections of individuals. Even though we think of corporations such as Apple, Ford Motors, or McDonald's as if they were monolithic entities and talk about them as if they were people in their own right, businesses are individuals all the way down, from the owners, to the CEO and board of directors, to the workers on the production line and those staffing the phones and washing the restrooms. Businesses are made up of individuals, usually working with other individuals, to create something bigger than themselves and engage in commerce with other businesses and individuals. They represent the autonomous choices of individuals to use their resources to pursue their multifaceted interests and, as such, they should be respected as any other individuals' should—especially when those individuals' interests, choices, and autonomy are endangered by the pursuit of the goals of society as a whole.

DEMOCRACY AND BALANCE

I've spent a lot of time criticizing ways in which the government fails to respect the rights, choices, and interests of individuals in their various roles (including as businesses). Does this leave any room for the government to actually *do* anything? Yes, it does, and in a way that does not limit the scale or scope of government, but rather *how* it does what it does.[66]

As always, a balance must be struck between the things that individuals collectively want their government to do and the limits, based on the rights and dignity of individuals, on how they may do it. Depending on their interests, the voters may direct their elected representatives to do more or less in certain areas, including education, national defense, health care, and funding for the arts. In Ronald Dworkin's terms, these are legitimate matters of policy to be deliberated in a representative body, typically a legislature charged with executing voters' political preferences. These are the typically boring debates in Congress or Parliament regarding funding bills and federal budgets that few watch voluntarily. But this is the essential work of a democracy, deliberating over what the government will do on behalf of the citizens using their money.

Just as important as this process of deliberation are the policies that legislators deliberate about. Ideally, the action of government should be motivated by the concerns of the voters as relayed through the people they elect, the referenda they support, and other communication, such as letters, phone calls, and protests as reported through the media. Of course, some of this communication is louder than others, such as that coming from special interests and lobbyists, but there's nothing wrong with this as long as this influence isn't corrupted by illicit financial dealings. Concerned citizens, whether on behalf of business interests, labor unions, or environmental groups, have as much right to contact their elected representatives as anyone else; what they do not have the right to do is corrupt the process with money, gifts, and quid pro quos. As with speech in general, we need more communication with our government rather than less (as well as politicians honorable enough to resist corruption).

It has become cliché to say that "government works for us," and this cliché has become empty because we don't do enough to enforce it. If we want our government to do certain things on our behalf, rather than doing things on behalf of those who run government (or those in corrupt relationships with them), it's our responsibility to let them know. Another aspect of the decline in our self-respect as individuals is that we don't take enough responsibility for telling our elected leaders what we do and do not want them to do. Just as Immanuel Kant said that our autonomy is both a capacity for independent choice and a responsibility to use it well, in the political sphere our responsibility is to make the government aware of what they should do on our behalf.

Regardless of the scale or scope of government the voters want, anything the government sets out to do must be accomplished while respecting the essential rights of individuals and only overriding them in cases of true emergency (which does not make them uncontroversial). If the government wants to increase the number of doctors in poorly served areas, they can't conscript medical students (or promising undergraduates) and send them where they are needed. Instead, the government can (and does) provide incentives for young doctors to go to such areas and then leaves the choices up to the doctors to decide who wants to participate. The balance between collective need and individual rights in this case is made in favor of individuals because there are other ways to meet the need without denying individuals their rights. In other cases, collective need will take precedence, such as military conscriptions during wartime, which is controversial nonetheless, but the need in that case is comprehensible even to those who oppose it. Conscription is an extreme case, though; more common are cases such as those mentioned throughout this book in which individual interests, choices, and autonomy were minimized or dismissed in the pursuit of collective goals.

In general, governments in liberal democracies should operate on the basis of *respect* and *responsiveness*: responding to the people's expressed concerns in ways that respect their rights as individuals. Such a guiding principle would preserve the government's role of serving the needs of the public, while making sure it does so in a way that doesn't threaten the rights of the individuals that make it up.[67] This is consistent with many visions for what or how much government is supposed to do, in that it is responsive to communication from its citizens on that regard, but also recognizes that those same citizens have rights that should not be set aside while solving problems. Many people want the government more involved in health care, for example, but that doesn't imply they want to give up all of their decision-making autonomy regarding their health care choices. Other people want the government to spend more on infrastructure, which may involve some reasonable takings of private property, but they don't want this done chiefly to benefit other private concerns. Just as individuals should respect the rights of others when pursuing their own interests, governments should respect the established rights of their citizens when pursuing policy goals, rather than lapsing into a tyranny of the majority in which rights are set aside in the interest of "progress."

This last concern speaks strongly against a culture of government in which "pragmatism" is the order of the day and national leaders and legislators focus on "getting things done" while dismissing concerns about due process and individual rights. Americans have been concerned for many years about deadlock in Washington with the executive and legislative branches split between the major parties, and their presidents responding to this by relying more and more on executive orders to do what would normally be done through the legislative process. I'm not arguing that this shift in process itself represents a greater danger to individual rights, except in the sense that the legislative process will usually result in a more thorough consideration of new laws, policies, and regulations, and any violation of individual rights is more likely to be flagged before implementation. (And in either case, the protection of individual rights is still the domain of the judiciary branch, which remains above the fray.) More troubling to me is the mindset of getting things done, or simply doing anything at all, which tends to favor achieving politically popular and expedient outcomes over the messy work of worrying about process that protects the rights of individuals. In this sense, "being pragmatic" is nothing more than a euphemism for sloppy utilitarian thinking that favors the short-term benefits from immediate action while disguising its long-term costs.

Conclusion

Most liberal democracies in the West embody the principle of protecting individual choice and interests while providing public services in response to citizen initiative, all against the background of their particular philosophies of governance. This has always been a balancing act and the balance reached varies from time to time and from country to country. Lately, however, the balance seems to be tipping farther in the direction that favors collective interests at the expense of those of the individual. In the early chapters of this book, I explained several possible reasons for this shift, including changes in the way we think of the workings of the brain, in ways we make decisions, and our behavior as individuals within a society, all of which point toward a diminished value and status of the individual. Not only does this enable the government to give less regard to the choices and interests of individuals, but it also leads us to have less faith in ourselves, which makes us more willing to accept the weakening of the protections of our interests. If this is indeed the cycle we are in, we need to put a stop to it by reaffirming, to ourselves and others, our value as individuals and demanding the respect we deserve as cognitively and morally competent persons with dignity.

Notes

1. See note 51 in chapter 3.
2. On the various meanings of the term "utility," see John Broome's parsimoniously titled article "Utility," *Economics & Philosophy* 7(1991): 1–12. For more on utilitarianism in general, I would suggest the essays in Ben Eggleston and Dale E. Miller (eds), *The Cambridge Companion to Utilitarianism* (Cambridge: Cambridge University Press, 2014).
3. This point has been made by John Rawls (*A Theory of Justice*, Cambridge, MA: Harvard University Press, 1971) and Bernard Williams (*Moral Luck*, Cambridge: Cambridge University Press, 1981). For more criticism of utilitarianism, see J.J.C. Smart and Bernard Williams, *Utilitarianism: For and Against* (Cambridge: Cambridge University Press, 1973) and Samuel Scheffler (ed.), *Consequentialism and Its Critics* (Oxford: Oxford University Press, 1988).
4. W.D. Ross, *The Right and the Good* (Oxford: Oxford University Press, 1930).
5. For an overview of deontology in all its variety, see Larry Alexander and Michael Moore, "Deontological Ethics," *Stanford Encyclopedia of*

Philosophy, October 17, 2016, at https://plato.stanford.edu/entries/ethics-deontological/.
6. Most of Kant's ethical thought can be found in *Grounding for the Metaphysics of Morals*, translated by James W. Ellington (Indianapolis, IN: Hackett Publishing Company, 1785/1993) and *The Metaphysics of Morals*, translated and edited by Mary J. Gregor (Cambridge: Cambridge University Press, 1797/1996). An excellent introduction is Roger J. Sullivan, *An Introduction to Kant's Ethics* (Cambridge: Cambridge University Press, 1994).
7. *Star Trek* references: 3. *Star Wars* references: 0. Take that, Sunstein!
8. The concept of utility monsters comes from Robert Nozick's *Anarchy, State, and Utopia* (New York: Basic Books, 1974), p. 41.
9. On threshold deontology, see Michael S. Moore, "Torture and the Balance of Evils," *Israel Law Review* 23(1989): 280–344; for criticism of the idea, see Larry Alexander, "Deontology at the Threshold," *University of San Diego Law Review* 37(2000): 893–912.
10. Ronald Dworkin, *Taking Rights Seriously* (Cambridge, MA: Harvard University Press, 1977), p. xi.
11. This derives from the Fifth Amendment to the Constitution, which says that no person shall "be deprived of life, liberty, or property, without due process of law; nor shall private property be taken for public use, without just compensation" (emphasis added). For more, see Richard A. Epstein, *Takings: Private Property and the Power of Eminent Domain* (Cambridge, MA: Harvard University Press, 1985) and Ilya Somin, *The Grasping Hand: Kelo v. City of New London and the Limits of Eminent Domain* (Chicago: University of Chicago Press, 2015).
12. For a summary of some of the worst abuses of eminent domain (as of 2002), see Dana Berliner, "Government Theft: The Top 10 Abuses of Eminent Domain," Institute for Justice, March 2002, at http://ij.org/report/government-theft/. The city of Pittsburgh, in particular, is well known for its use of eminent domain for questionable purposes; see, for instance, John Tierney, "Your Land Is My Land," *The New York Times*, July 5, 2005, at http://www.nytimes.com/2005/07/05/opinion/your-land-is-my-land.html. President Donald Trump also benefited from eminent domain while a private citizen; see Ilya Somin, "Donald Trump's History of Eminent Domain Abuse," *The Washington Post*, August 19, 2015, at https://www.washingtonpost.com/news/volokh-conspiracy/wp/2015/08/19/donald-trumps-abuse-of-eminent-domain (and of this writing, he plans to use it as president to claim land for his wall at the U.S.-Mexico border).
13. *Kelo v. City of New London*, 545 U.S. 469 (2005). For the story behind the case, see Jeff Benedict, *Little Pink House: A True Story of Defiance and*

Courage (New York: Grand Central Publishing, 2009), and for more on the case itself, see Somin, *Grasping Hand*, and Richard A. Epstein, "Public Use in a Post-*Kelo* World," *Supreme Court Economic Review* 17(2009): 151–171.
14. *Kelo*, 545 U.S. at 488. The use of the term "efficiency" coincides with the treatment of rights in the *economic approach to law*, in which rights are valuable only insofar as they maximize total utility; insofar as parties refuse to engage in an "obviously" value-enhancing transaction, judges are encouraged to "mimic the market" and reassign property rights to lead to greater "efficiency." (See my book *Kantian Ethics and Economics: Autonomy, Dignity, and Character*, Stanford, CA: Stanford University Press, 2011, pp. 146–154, for more.)
15. Somin, *Grasping Hand*, p. 24. The cases cited above are *Berman v. Parker*, 348 U.S. 26 (1954) and *Hawaii Housing Authority v. Midkiff*, 467 U.S. 229 (1984).
16. *Kelo*, 545 U.S. at 503.
17. Ibid. at 505; see Somin, *Grasping Hand*, pp. 127–131, for more on O'Connor's dissent.
18. Not popularly enough, judging from the number of people surveyed after the 2016 election who wanted to repeal Obamacare but keep the ACA. See Kyle Dropp and Brendan Nyhan, "One-Third Don't Know Obamacare and Affordable Care Act Are the Same," *The New York Times*, February 7, 2017, at https://www.nytimes.com/2017/02/07/upshot/one-third-dont-know-obamacare-and-affordable-care-act-are-the-same.html.
19. For more details on the ACA, see Purva H. Rawal, *The Affordable Act: Examining the Facts* (Santa Barbara, CA: ABC-CLIO, 2016).
20. On the public nature of health and health care, see John Coggan, *What Makes Health Public? A Critical Evaluation of Moral, Legal, and Political Claims in Public Health* (Cambridge: Cambridge University Press, 2012).
21. See Randy E. Barnett, "Commandeering the People: Why the Individual Health Insurance Mandate Is Unconstitutional," *N.Y.U. Journal of Law & Liberty* 5(2010): 581–637, and Randy E. Barnett, Nathaniel Stewart, and Todd Gaziano, "Why the Personal Mandate to Buy Health Insurance is Unprecedented and Unconstitutional," The Heritage Foundation (2009), at http://www.heritage.org/health-care-reform/report/why-the-personal-mandate-buy-health-insurance-unprecedented-and. For more on Barnett and his efforts on this point, see Josh Blackman's book *Unprecedented: The Constitutional Challenge to Obamacare* (New York: PublicAffairs, 2013), especially Barnett's forward, and Sheryl Gay Stolberg and Charlie Savage, "Vindication for Challenger of Health Care Law," *The New York Times*, March 26, 2012, at http://www.nytimes.com/2012/03/27/us/randy-barnetts-pet-cause-end-of-health-law-hits-supreme-court.html.

22. Article I, Section 8, Clause 3, of the U.S. Constitution.
23. The case did attract an admirable amount of interest from legal scholars and philosophers very quickly; for example, see Nathaniel Persily, Gillian E. Metzger, and Trevor W. Morrison (eds), *The Health Care Case: The Supreme Court's Decision and Its Implications* (Oxford: Oxford University Press, 2013) and Fritz Allhoff and Mark Hall (eds), *The Affordable Care Act Decision: Philosophical and Legal Implications* (New York: Routledge, 2014).
24. *National Federation of Independent Business v. Sebelius*, 567 U.S. 519 (2012).
25. Ibid., at 21.
26. Ibid., at 23.
27. Ibid., at 58 (emphasis mine).
28. See Randy E. Barnett, "No Small Feat: Who Won the Health Care Case (and Why Did So Many Law Professors Miss the Boat)?", *Florida Law Review* 65 (2013): 1331–1350.
29. In fact, this was mentioned by Chief Justice Roberts in his opinion: "Indeed, the Government's logic would justify a mandatory purchase to solve almost any problem. ... [For example] many Americans do not eat a balanced diet. ... The failure of that group to have a healthy diet increases health care costs... [which] are borne in part by other Americans who must pay more, just as the uninsured shift costs to the insured. ... Congress addressed the insurance problem by ordering everyone to buy insurance. Under the Government's theory, Congress could ddress the diet problem by ordering everyone to buy vegetables" (*NFIB v. Sebelius*, 567 U.S. (2012), at 22–23).
30. Note, for instance, James R. Baumgardner and colleagues' study of tobacco use that lists the impact of changes in smoking rates on various elements of the federal budget: lower smoking decreases Medicare and Medicaid expenditures to treat smoking-related diseases, but it increases Social Security and Medicare outlays through people living longer. See Baumgardner et al., "Cigarette Taxes and the Federal Budget—Report from the CBO," *The New England Journal of Medicine* 367(2012): 2068–2070.
31. *District of Columbia v. Heller*, 554 U.S. 570 (2008). For a debate over the decision and its implications, see "After *Heller*: The New Debate About Guns," *CATO Unbound*, July 2008, at https://www.cato-unbound.org/issues/july-2008/after-heller-new-american-debate-about-guns.
32. *Citizens United v. Federal Election Commission*, 558 U.S. 310 (2010).
33. The *Heller* decision was met with predictable and understandable opposition from gun-control activists, but also from the American Civil Liberties Union, which "interprets the Second Amendment as a collective right"

(Suzanne Ito, "*Heller* Decision and the Second Amendment," ACLU.org, July 1, 2008, at https://www.aclu.org/blog/speakeasy/heller-decision-and-second-amendment). With respect to *Citizens United*, see Liz Kennedy, "10 Ways *Citizens United* Endangers Democracy," *Demos*, January 19, 2012, at http://www.demos.org/publication/10-ways-citizens-united-endangers-democracy; Jeffrey Toobin, "Money Unlimited," *The New Yorker*, May 21, 2012, at http://www.newyorker.com/magazine/2012/05/21/money-unlimited; and David Cole, "How to Reverse *Citizens United*," *The Atlantic*, April 2016, at https://www.theatlantic.com/magazine/archive/2016/04/how-to-reverse-citizens-united/471504/.

34. On the history of this quote and possible sources for it, see the Quote Investigator, June 1, 2015, at http://quoteinvestigator.com/2015/06/01/defend-say/.
35. *Schenck v. United States*, 249 U.S. 47 (1919). On the fascinating history of this case and Holmes' opinions about free speech and individual rights in general, see Thomas Healy, *The Great Dissent: How Oliver Wendell Holmes Changes His Mind—and Changed the History of Free Speech in America* (New York: Metropolitan, 2013).
36. *Schenck v. United States*, 249 U.S. 47, at 52. For more on this, see Trevor Timm, "It's Time to Stop Using the 'Fire in Crowded Theatre' Quote," *The Atlantic*, November 2, 2012, at https://www.theatlantic.com/national/archive/2012/11/its-time-to-stop-using-the-fire-in-a-crowded-theater-quote/264449/.
37. *Brandenburg v. Ohio*, 395 U.S. 444 (1969).
38. For more, see Erwin Chemerinsky and Howard Gillman, *Free Speech on Campus* (New Haven: Yale University Press, 2017).
39. Treating offense as serious harm is not a new idea; see, for instance, Joel Feinberg, *Offense to Others* (Oxford: Oxford University Press, 1985).
40. John Stuart Mill, *On Liberty* (London: Walter Scott Pub. Co., 1859), pp. 30–31, available at http://www.gutenberg.org/ebooks/34901.
41. Ulrich Baer, "What 'Snowflakes' Get Right About Free Speech," *The New York Times*, April 24, 2017, at https://www.nytimes.com/2017/04/24/opinion/what-liberal-snowflakes-get-right-about-free-speech.html.
42. This is not to mention the increasingly frequent use of violence to interrupt campus speakers, which is inexcusable.
43. Mill, *On Liberty*, pp. 39–40.
44. Conor Friedersdorf, "What an NYU Administrator Got Wrong about Campus Speech," *The Atlantic*, April 27, 2017, at https://www.theatlantic.com/politics/archive/2017/04/what-an-nyu-administrator-got-wrong-about-campus-speech/524442/.

45. See Mill's *On Liberty*, chapter 1. Although I focus on tyrannies of the majority on the part of the government, Mill was concerned about more conventional (as opposed to legal) pressures as well: "Society can and does execute its own mandates: and if it issues wrong mandates instead of right, or any mandates at all in things with which it ought not to meddle, it practices a social tyranny more formidable than many kinds of political oppression, since, though not usually upheld by such extreme penalties, it leaves fewer means of escape, penetrating much more deeply into the details of life, and enslaving the soul itself" (p. 8).
46. Laws banning interracial marriage were declared unconstitutional in *Loving v. Virginia* (388 U.S. 1, 1967), as were laws banning same-sex marriage in *Obergefell v. Hodges* (576 U.S. ___, 2015). (More on the latter soon.).
47. *Plessy v. Ferguson* (163 U.S. 537, 1896); *Korematsu v. United States* (323 U.S. 214, 1944).
48. Most of what we will discuss is found in Dworkin, *Taking Rights Seriously*, especially chapter 4, "Hard Cases."
49. On this debate, see Robert W. Bennett and Lawrence B. Solum, *Constitutional Originalism: A Debate* (Ithaca, NY: Cornell University Press, 2011).
50. *Brown v. Board of Education of Topeka*, 347 U.S. 483 (1954); *Boumediene v. Bush*, 553 U.S. 723 (2008).
51. For more on the law and politics of same-sex marriage, see Evan Gerstmann, *Same-Sex Marriage and the Constitution*, 3rd ed. (Cambridge: Cambridge University Press, 2017).
52. Unfortunately, even the author of *On Liberty* was confused on this point, writing that "individual liberty is not involved in the doctrine of Free Trade" (p. 180). The persistence of this distinction to this day reflects a long-standing disdain for economic matters (dismissed as commercial, mercantile, or "bourgeois") dating back for centuries. No one has done more to explore and explain the changing attitudes toward the marketplace throughout history than economist, philosopher, and historian Deirdre McCloskey; see her trilogy of *The Bourgeois Virtues: Ethics for an Age of Commerce* (2006), *Bourgeois Dignity: Why Economics Can't Explain the Modern World* (2010), and *Bourgeois Equality: How Ideas, Not Capital or Institutions, Enriched the World* (2016), all published by University of Chicago Press.
53. For such a view, see Nozick, *Anarchy, State, and Utopia*, Part II.
54. If this sounds like Dworkin's judges balancing principles in hard cases, I agree; I argue for a Dworkinian model of judgment within Kantian ethics in my paper "Judgment: Balancing Principle and Policy," *Review of Social Economy* 73(2015): 223–241.

55. See *Fortune* magazine's list of "The 100 Best Companies to Work For," which of as May 2017 listed Google and Wegman's as number one and two, respectively: http://beta.fortune.com/best-companies/.
56. Milton Friedman, "The Social Responsibility of Business Is To Increase Its Profits," *New York Times Sunday Magazine*, September 13, 1970, p. 32 (available at http://www.colorado.edu/studentgroups/libertarians/issues/friedman-soc-resp-business.html). For a critical look at Friedman's claims, see Martin Calkins and Jonathan B. Wight, "The Ethical Lacunae in Friedman's Concept of the Manager," *Journal of Markets & Morality* 11 (2008): 221–238.
57. For instance, see the seminal work in corporate social responsibility (CSR), Howard R. Bowen, *Social Responsibilities of the Businessman* (Iowa City, IA: University of Iowa Press, 1953), as well as more recent work, such as Renginee Pillay, *The Changing Nature of Corporate Social Responsibility: CSR and Development in Context—The Case of Mauritius* (Abingdon, UK: Routledge, 2015).
58. This analysis of the nature of limited liability is disputed; see, for instance, Stephen Kinsella, "Corporate Personhood, Limited Liability, and Double Taxation," *The Libertarian Standard*, October 18, 2011, at http://libertarianstandard.com/2011/10/18/corporate-personhood-limited-liability-and-double-taxation/.
59. This is a controversial point, of course, especially among those who see the rise of the corporation as a net negative social force. On the history of the corporation in the United States and the debates over its effects, see Naomi R. Lamoreaux and William J. Novak (eds), *Corporations and American Democracy* (Cambridge, MA: Harvard University Press, 2017).
60. *Burwell v. Hobby Lobby Stores, Inc.*, 573 U.S. ___ (2014). In its 2017 term (starting in October), the Court will hear the case of a baker who refused his services for a same-sex wedding (*Masterpiece v. Colorado Civil Rights Commission*).
61. For an argument in favor of religious liberty if alternative opportunities for the denied service exist, see Richard A. Epstein, "The War Against Religious Liberty," *Defining Ideas*, April 7, 2015, at http://www.hoover.org/research/war-against-religious-liberty. On the question of whether religious belief should receive special treatment (compared to secular convictions), see Brian Leiter's provocatively titled *Why Tolerate Religion?* (Princeton: Princeton University Press, 2012). On the issues with the ACA in particular, see Josh Blackman, *Unraveled: Obamacare, Religious Liberty, and Executive Power* (Cambridge: Cambridge University Press, 2016).
62. For example, see my article "On the Justification of Antitrust: A Matter of Rights and Wrongs," *The Antitrust Bulletin* 61(2016): 323–335, as well as my exchange with Ryan Long and Alan M. Barr in the same issue.

63. *Lochner v. New York*, 198 U.S. 45 (1905). On the case and its legacy, see David E. Bernstein, *Rehabilitating* Lochner*: Defending Individual Rights against Progressive Reform* (Chicago: University of Chicago Press, 2011).
64. *Citizens United v. Federal Election Commission*, 558 U.S. 310 (2010), at p. 7 of Justice Scalia's concurrence.
65. This is not to ignore the difficulty of determining legal responsibility of individuals within groups such as corporations. For example, when a corporation is found liable for harm, whether civil or criminal, what person or group of persons is actually held responsible? On this, see Catherine P. Wells, "Corrective Justice and Corporate Tort Liability," *Southern California Law Review* 69(1996): 1769–1780 (available at http://lawdigitalcommons.bc.edu/cgi/viewcontent.cgi?article=1466&context=lsfp), and Celia Wells, *Corporations and Criminal Responsibility*, 2nd ed, (Oxford: Oxford University Press, 2001).
66. Much of what follows was discussed at more length in the final chapter of my book, *The Illusion of Well-Being: Economic Policymaking Based on Respect and Responsiveness* (New York: Palgrave Macmillan, 2014).
67. A related problem, beyond the scope of the present book, is the tendency of governments to "find" problems in statistics, such as economic output or "gross national happiness" data, rather than responding to those raised directly by its citizens. (This was the focus of the first half of *The Illusion of Well-Being*.)

CHAPTER 6

Conclusion

In this book, I've argued that there are signs of a steady decline in respect for the individual in modern society. This can be seen in how we interpret breaking developments in psychology and neuroscience: when a new limitation on cognitive capacity or deviation from preconceived notions of rationality are discovered, the conclusion is often that individuals are doomed to be poor decision-makers, rather than recognizing that these "flaws" have always existed. We were never perfect, rational thinkers, but in the context of our complex and multifaceted interests, we might be doing just fine. In any case, there is no way to say for sure that we aren't making good choices without stacking the deck against us by assuming a wildly unrealistic capacity for rational thought to begin with, a straw man that is often put forward by those who benefit from knocking it down.

We also see increasing doubts about the moral competency of the individual from the side of the humanities, particularly from those who also adhere to a caricature of the individual who can only make decisions in his or her own selfish interests, implying that only the benevolent hand of government can ensure that the interests of the whole aren't ignored in individuals' pursuit of their own narrowly defined goals. Once again, those who believe we are in a state of "radical individualism" are often those who stand to gain by using it to argue for the other extreme, a completely collectivized society in which the select few (including them, of course) make decisions for the benefit of the rest of us.

This misunderstanding suggests a stark conflict between the individual and society, which is a false dichotomy. We are essentially individuals, each of us of a single and unique mind; it's what we are, it's how we make decisions, and it's how we interact with other individuals in the world. There is nothing in our uniqueness and distinctiveness that implies the content of our choices must be focused on our individual selves. Human beings are, by and large, an incredibly compassionate and altruistic species, by both evolved and cultivated sentiment. This can be difficult to remember amid the atrocities committed by the human race every day, but these are aberrations, as shown by the reaction of the many to the heinous acts of the few.

All these developments reflect and reinforce the decline in regard for the individual and encourage the trend in policymaking toward neglecting their rights. According to this view, rights are only as important as those who make use of them, and if individuals are not cognitively or morally competent to make use of their rights to the benefit of themselves or those around them, it is not important to protect them. Why value the individual's right to decline health insurance or a retirement savings plan if those are considered to be bad decisions? Why protect an individual's property right if she doesn't agree it's worth selling her house or land when the government makes her a good offer? Why protect the individual's right to free speech if they're just going to say things that upset other people?

The irony here is that we're limiting the rights of individuals ostensibly for their own sake, implying that rights are less important than interests. However, the value of an individual's interests is based on the rights, and ultimately the dignity, of the individual. If persons have no rights, no dignity, and no value, their interests will not matter, but only their well-being as others perceive it. This way of thinking about persons reduces them to mere animals that we care for but do not respect. This is not the way governments should regard their citizens, but this is the inevitable result of a continuing decline in respect for the individual.

While I argue for a restoration of the status of the individual vis-à-vis society, I do not argue for the individual's superiority. This is not a book about individualism, but rather about the individual or individuality. While one person alone can do incredible things, we can do so much more by working together. We don't always get along, but for the most part the people around us help us prosper and flourish. Society is, at its core, a group of individuals, and if we forget that, we are missing the trees for the forest. The whole may be greater than the sum of its parts, but without the parts the whole is nothing.

Government plays a role here too, provided that role is limited to protecting the rights of individuals—from each other as well as from the state itself—and responding to the legitimate needs of the people in a way that both supports and respect them. As with my previous books *The Manipulation of Choice* and *The Illusion of Well-Being*, I believe the message in this book can resonate with people across the mainstream political spectrum. What I've described is consistent with the full range of opinions regarding the scale and scope of government activity, from the minimal government of libertarians and some conservatives to the more expansive state of liberals (and some other conservatives). What I've emphasized is that the government should consider and protect the rights of the individual while pursuing their policy goals. This does not mean the rights of the individual must always trump policy concerns, but certainly more often than they have lately. This is the declared and acknowledged stance of most Western liberal democracies, regardless of the political party in power at any certain time. All I'm asking is for them to do it *better*, to acknowledge and resist the decline in respect for the individual that is inherent in their collectivist mindset and reflected in their political and judicial decisions.

Finally, I'm urging all of us to embrace our own individuality and resist the trend from many quarters in society to deny it. Each of us can do this, but I sincerely hope we can do it together.

Index

A

Algorithms, 3, 31, 32, 40, 45–57, 63, 65, 67, 68
Altruism, 35, 72, 73, 96, 105
Authenticity, 30, 47, 48, 84, 86, 89–91
Autonomy, 30, 34, 36, 47, 72, 77–82, 84, 86, 88–96, 100, 102, 104, 110, 132, 138–140, 143

B

Behavioral economics, 14, 15, 33, 36
Big Data, 3, 31, 40, 42, 45, 50, 51, 53–58, 65–67
Brooks, David, 74–79, 90, 91, 100, 101, 104, 106
Business, 3, 8, 31, 39, 42, 45–48, 51, 53, 54, 57, 60, 62, 68, 71, 91, 111, 117, 118, 132–139, 144, 147

C

Choice, 1–4, 7–12, 14–30, 32–37, 42, 47–52, 58, 60, 62, 63, 71, 72, 74, 76–84, 86, 88, 89, 91–93, 95–98, 101, 102, 107, 108, 112, 117–119, 121, 126, 130, 131, 133, 136–141, 149–151
Criminal justice, 53, 55, 67

D

Decision-making, 1, 2, 4, 5, 7, 8, 10–15, 17, 18, 22–26, 29–31, 35, 40, 42–44, 47, 52, 54, 62, 67, 71, 93, 96, 97, 101, 109–112, 133, 140
Deontology, 102, 108–110, 112, 113, 141, 142
Duty, 86, 94–96, 110, 112

E

Economics, 7, 11, 12, 14, 15, 31–36, 59, 65, 68, 72, 75–77, 100–102, 105, 112, 131, 141, 143, 146
Existentialism, 83, 102

G

Government, 2, 3, 5, 8, 17, 21, 28, 31, 34, 36, 39, 42, 45, 47, 48, 53, 54, 56, 57, 60, 62, 68, 71–73, 75, 87, 91, 96, 111, 113–121, 125, 127–129, 131–135, 137–142, 144, 146, 148–151

H

Happiness, 1–4, 11, 22, 26, 27, 31, 34, 39, 40, 44, 56, 61, 63, 68, 69, 73, 75, 90, 108, 128, 148

I

Individual, 2–5, 7, 8, 11, 15, 17–21, 23, 24, 26–31, 40, 42, 45, 48, 50, 52, 55–64, 71–83, 85, 87–92, 94–98, 107–109, 112, 113–115, 119, 121, 131, 136, 137, 149–151

Interests, 2, 4, 5, 9, 12, 13, 16–24, 26–31, 34, 35, 40, 42, 44–49, 51, 52, 58, 61–63, 71, 72, 79, 80, 84, 89, 90, 92, 93, 95, 97, 99, 107, 108, 111, 113–115, 117–122, 125–127, 129–134, 136–141, 149, 150

K

Kant, Immanuel, 4, 5, 25, 30, 36, 60, 68, 69, 72, 79, 80, 93, 99, 105, 108, 110, 139

M

Mill, John Stuart, 5, 61, 69, 82, 102, 104, 108, 123, 125, 145

N

Neuroscience, 3, 4, 7, 11, 14, 31, 32, 36, 37, 42, 47, 57, 58, 62, 71, 99, 100, 149

P

Politics, 3, 34, 57, 65, 69, 73, 75, 88–90, 99, 104, 107, 131, 146

Preferences, 12, 21–23, 29, 35, 37, 63, 76, 77, 81, 82, 86, 92, 108, 126–128, 130, 132, 136, 138

Principles, 22, 23, 27, 51, 69, 89, 110, 112, 113, 127–129, 132, 146

Psychology, 3, 4, 7, 11, 14, 15, 31–33, 42, 57, 58, 62, 65, 71, 75, 85, 86, 99, 100, 103, 149

Q

Quantification, 3, 31, 39, 40, 43, 44, 50, 51, 56–58, 60–62, 67–69, 91

R

Rights, 5, 22, 40, 60–62, 67, 89, 94, 107, 108, 110–132, 136–140, 142, 143, 145–148, 150, 151

Roles, 45, 78, 83, 86–88, 138

S

Sociality, 64, 73, 79, 100, 101

Society, 2–5, 24, 31, 42, 43, 54, 56–58, 61–63, 65–67, 72–75, 77, 79, 84, 89–92, 96–99, 107, 108, 111, 113, 114, 119, 121, 123, 125, 127, 128, 131, 134, 135, 137, 141, 146, 149–151

Supreme Court, 5, 78, 114–116, 118, 120, 122, 126–130, 132, 136, 137, 143, 144

U

Utilitarianism, 35, 61, 62, 69, 102, 108–113, 141

Printed in the United States
By Bookmasters